HE STORY OF WALWORTH

with the Elephant and Castle, Newingto

This booklet is a brief, simple, introduction to the history of one part of the London Borough of Southwark. It is written mainly for readers whose homes or schools are in that part of Southwark which stretches from New Kent Road to Albany Road, Kennington Park Road to Old Kent Road. It overlaps with Neighbourhood Histories, 1, 3, 7 & 8. Suggestions for further reading are given. Some are available at, or through, any Southwark library and a few are in print but anyone wishing to make a more detailed or advanced study should visit the Southwark Local Studies Library, 211 Borough High Street, London SE1, Tel.071-403-3507. This has a comprehensive collection of books, maps, illustrations, press-cuttings, archives and microfilms (of census returns, local newspapers etc.) covering all parts of the London Borough of Southwark. The opening hours may be obtained from any library. An appointment in advance is helpful and is essential for consultation of the archives, use of the microfilm reader, or for school party visits.

Cover Illustration *The Elephant and Castle, 1826*
Inside Front Cover *Plan of the Manor of Walworth, 1681*
ISBN   0 – 905849 – 10 – 8

THE STORY OF
WALWORTH

CONTENTS

. WALWORTH ROAD - A JOURNEY BACK IN TIME

If your home is between the Elephant and Castle and Burgess Park, or between Old Kent Road and Kennington Park Road, you live in Walworth. The centre of this neighbourhood is Walworth Road, a main route into central London and also one long shopping street for the many thousands who live in the smaller streets and big housing estates on either side of it.

It is difficult to imagine a time when this was not a noisy, crowded neighbourhood. Yet there are clues to point you on a long journey back through the centuries to a very different Walworth. In the Cuming Museum, Walworth Road, are bones and teeth of a mammoth, a prehistoric hairy elephant, found in a bed of sand twelve feet below the surface of Hillingdon Street, and also the backbone of a woolly rhinoceros discovered during road works in Old Kent Road. If you live in one of the tall blocks of flats, look out from your window and try to imagine Walworth when these strange creatures may have roamed here. As you see the ground is very flat, no hills to block the view. In early times, this was marshy ground, flooded at times by the River Thames. Islands of sand and gravel rose above the surrounding mud. Many streams and ditches are marked on early maps before the neighbourhood was built up, though now of course they have long been hidden in sewers underground. It is not known who were the earliest human residents of Walworth but, in 1988, archaeologists working on a site near Marcia Road, just east of Old Kent Road, uncovered a large wooden platform, made by piling branches on top of each other, which they believe was made by Stone Age people about 4,500 years ago. It is the only one of its kind found in London. In 1990 so many worked flints were found in an excavation between Bowles Road and Old Kent Road that archaeologists believe it was a Stone Age tool-making site.

The Romans certainly knew the Walworth area as it lies between two Roman roads to 'Londinium'. Kennington Park Road, Newington Butts and Newington Causeway follow the line of Stane Street from Chichester and the Sussex coast. Old Kent Road and its continuation, Tabard Street, earlier known as Kent Street, are more or less on the line of Watling Street.

The flints, mentioned above, lay under a section of this road which had bee uncovered by the archaeologists. Legionaries who landed at Dover marche to London by way of Watling Street. A stone head of the Roman god, Janus was found about three hundred years ago, somewhere near Old Ker Road. After the Romans left, the Anglo-Saxons came to Britain. Perhaps because of the marshy ground, the local Britons were not all driven fror their homes by these invaders. The Anglo-Saxons called the neighbourhoo Wealawyrd, or Waleorde, meaning 'the farm of the Britons'. With som changes in spelling the name is still the same today - Walworth. Wales an Cornwall take their names from the same Anglo-Saxon word.

An important event in Walworth's very early history is recorded in th archives of Lambeth Palace, London residence of the Archbishop c Canterbury. The manuscript tells how a jester, named Hitard, wh entertained at the court of the Anglo-Saxon king, Edmund, perhaps Edmun of Wessex, who reigned from 934 to 946, pleased the king, so he made hin a grant of land, a place called Wealawyrd, that is, Walworth. Hitar (sometimes spelt Nithard) later went on pilgrimage to Rome, to pray at th places where St Peter and St Paul were martyred, a long and dangerou journey in those days. Before setting out he made over his land in Walwort to 'the Church of Christ in Canterbury', Canterbury Cathedral. The proceed of the land were used 'for the clothing of the monks'. All through th centuries the Cathedral continued to own Walworth, right down to 186: when it passed to the Church Commissioners. Now, after about a thousan years, thanks to a jester's gift, parts of Walworth still belong to the church Look out for the letters E.C.E., Ecclesiastical (Church) Commissioners o England, over houses in Liverpool Grove.

References and further reading

1. E.J.Orford, ed. - *The Book of Walworth*, Browning Hall Adult School 1925
2. *Survey of London, Vol.xxv, St George's Fields, the parishes of St George the Martyr, Southwark and St Mary Newington. L.C.C., 1955.* pp 1-2.
3. Wendy Rogers - *Mesolithic and Neolithic flint tool-manufacturing areas buried beneath Roman Watling Street in Southwark,* London Archaeologist Vol. 6, no. 9, 1990.

For more detailed study -
4.   Margaret Gelling - *Early charters of the Thames Valley*, Leicester University Press,1979.

2.   THE MANOR OF WALWORTH AND PARISH OF ST MARY NEWINGTON

> Baynard holds Walworth from the Archbishop. Before 1066 it was for the clothing of the monks, – Land for 3 ploughs. In the lord's demesne 1 plough; 14 villagers and 5 small holders with 3 ploughs. There is a church. Meadow, 8 acres.

Domesday Book, 1086

Not many places can trace their history as far back as Walworth. Mostly the first mention is in Domesday Book, compiled for King William the Conqueror in 1086. The entry for Walworth in Domesday Book, gives some picture of the village, or manor, of Walworth as it was 900 years ago, with its land for ploughing and growing corn and its meadowland for cows. For hundreds of years Walworth remained just such a small country village.

A map of the manor, made in 1681, for the Dean and Chapter of Canterbury Cathedral, shows only a few houses along 'Walworth Street', the village high street which has now become Walworth Road. At the centre of the village was a cross- roads. A lane leading to the fields on the east, still known to most local people as 'East Lane', is now officially, East Street. What was once West Lane is now Penrose Street. The Archbishop of Canterbury and his household, on their way to and from Lambeth Palace, could have used a short cut across the fields from Old Kent Road to Lambeth Road. It is marked on the map as 'King's Highway'. Kings had the right to use this route when travelling to Westminster. About where Alexander Fleming House now stands, there was a great gateway across the road. All traces of the gateway and the King's Highway have long since been lost. It was replaced in 1751 by the 'New' Kent Road. A 'New Town' that was to become Newington had much earlier grown up at the road junction which is now the Elephant and Castle. The earliest mention of it that has been traced, is in a document of 1212, 'Newington Street' is now the main road called Newington Butts.

In 1681 the land to the south of Newington Street and on either side of Walworth Road was just fields. The map shows the 'common fields', still partly divided into strips among the tenants of the Manor, as they had been in the Middle Ages. The fields were surrounded by earth walls. Brandon Street is on the line of one of these. Corn grown in the fields was taken to the mill to be ground into flour. A map by John Rocque, 1746, shows one windmill to the west of Newington Causeway. 'Windmill Lane', now Bethwin Road, led to another. The Windmill pub in Wyndham Road is a reminder of it. There were sheep and chickens. The *Accounts of Walworth Manor* in the Canterbury Cathedral archives mention income from wool and poultry. Some people kept bees. About the time of King John the queen's goldsmith paid a gallon of honey as rent for an acre of land in Newington. According to the *Court Leet Book of the Manor of Walworth*, in the 18th century everyone in Walworth had the right to keep 'two kine', that is cows, and one 'jade'; or horse, on Walworth Common. Today about 8,000 people live on that Common. It is covered by the huge blocks of flats of the Aylesbury Estate. To the west of Walworth Street was another common called the Lower Moor or Lorrimore, spelt Lattammore on the map of 1681 just north of where Lorrimore Square is today. An old meaning of moor was marshy ground. There was a large fishpond on Lorrimore Common.

The Lord of the Manor was the Dean and Chapter (clergy) of Canterbury Cathedral. Their lessee lived at the Manor House which was where today Manor Place crosses Penton Place. There are no known pictures of the old house, demolished in 1786, but there are descriptions of it in the Cathedral archives. There was a hall, or large room, where the lord and his lady and their servants ate, an upper room for the lord and his family, and a kitchen. Nearby was a great barn to store grain, a stable and a dovecote. At the entrance to the lord's 'demesne' was a great gate with a room over it. In Walworth Street just north of West Lane was the Lord's pound. Cows, sheep, or pigs found wandering would be put in the pound.

The Lord of the Manor had the right to hold courts and his clerk, or steward, kept notes, in Latin, on rolls of parchment. Some *Court Rolls of Walworth Manor* are preserved in the Public Record Office in London. There are many references to brewers, who probably made their beer from barley grown in local fields, and did good business with thirsty travellers on the main roads to London. In May 1336 the aletaster for Newington brought to court Martin le Meleward, who was fined 6 pence, maybe for charging too much or giving short measure. Incidentally, this seems to have been a trade in which women had equality even in the Middle Ages. The Christian names of three of the brewers fined at this time were Agnes, Juliana, and Alice!

Life on the Manor of Walworth was not all work. On May Day there would be dancing round the maypole, which can be seen on the 1681 map, set up in the middle of the 'King's Highway to Southwark', Newington Causeway. For a few years, about 1580-1594, Newington even had its own theatre, probably rather like Shakespeare's own theatre, the Globe, not far away on Bankside. When England was at war the English archers were famous for their skill with the longbow. King Henry VII ordered butts to be set up in the fields near London for bowmen to practise shooting. Possibly this is how Newington Butts got its name. The first reference to the name, which has been traced, is in 1512.

On Sundays and 'holy days' the people of Walworth went to church. There was a church here even in the time of Domesday Book. The site of this Saxon church, is not known, possibly it was near the Manor House, but from at least 1212 there are records of a church at Newington. The Manor of Walworth became the Parish of St Mary Newington. Their boundaries were the same. The church is marked on the 1681 map in what was then Newington Street. Over the years, the church was rebuilt several times, the last time in the 1790's. Next to it, was the Rectory, or Parsonage House, built of wood and plaster and surrounded by a moat with four bridges. By 1876, traffic had already increased so much, that church and rectory were finally demolished to widen the road. The old churchyard, once full of tombs with memorials to local people, is now a small park next to the Elephant and Castle Leisure Centre. The road beside the park is still called Churchyard

Row. The church itself was rebuilt a short distance away, on the other side of Kennington Park Road, but in 1941 this Victorian church, all except the tower, was burnt out in an air-raid. Now, however, a light modern building, behind the tower, carries on the worship and work of the church of St Mary Newington.

In the old days it was the custom once a year, to 'beat the bounds', that is to walk in procession round the boundaries of the parish, noting the boundary marks, beginning at the windmill, in what is now Bethwin Road East of Walworth Road, Boundary Lane still marks the old boundary with Camberwell. The parish extended north as far as the junction of Borough High Street and Long Lane including what is now, Trinity Church Square marked on the 1681 plan as 'Trinitie Land'.

Before there was any Borough Council the people of St Mary Newington parish managed their own affairs, by a committee known as the Vestry because it met originally in the Vestry of the Parish Church. The *Vestry Minutes*, which are now in the Southwark Archives, begin with a meeting held in 1583, over 400 years ago, during the reign of Queen Elizabeth I. It was the duty of the parish to collect a Poor Rate from all householders to provide for the poor, the old, the sick and the unemployed who could not find work to keep themselves. The Ratebooks with lists of householders and the amount each one paid, based on the value of his property, are also in the Archives. The earliest is for the year 1673. As maps show, the area north of the Elephant and Castle, near to central London, was built up early and even by 1770 the Parish of St Mary Newington was said to be 'burdened with numerous and expensive poor', (expensive, that is, to the ratepayers) An Act of Parliament allowed Walworth Common to be enclosed and let for building; the rents to be used for the relief of the poor. That is how Walworth lost its largest public open space. Other old South London villages kept their commons, Kennington Park, Peckham Rye, Clapham and Streatham commons.

The parish arranged for orphans and poor children to become apprentices For seven years, while they were learning a trade, they worked for a master with no pay, just food, clothes and lodging. There are many apprenticeship indentures (agreements) in the archives. In the early years the master was usually a local man. Later, when Newington had many poor people, sadly some of the children were sent far away, to the cotton and woollen mills of northern England. On a happier note, in 1710, long before there were any state schools, some people of St Mary Newington subscribed to start a school for poor children, who otherwise had no chance of any learning. St Mary Newington School stood until 1965 on the site of the Elephant and Castle Leisure Centre.

Other charitable people made some provision for old people. In 1642 John Walter, Clerk to the Drapers' Company in the City, built almshouses in St Mary Newington parish, and also in the next parish, St George the Martyr, because, as he said, many of the poor, 'had lately perished by lying abroad (outdoors) in the cold for want of habitation, to the great dishonour of God'. Homelessness is obviously no new problem. The Newington almshouses

Girls at St Mary Newington School, 1911

were demolished when the whole Elephant and Castle area was redeveloped. Draper House, a tall block of flats, has been named after them. However John Walter's Charity, begun 350 years ago, did not come to an end. In 1961 beautiful new homes for old people, called Walter's Close, were built in Brandon Street. With a clock tower and a courtyard garden they look very much like the almshouses of long ago. St Mary Newington Close, Surrey Square, is another home for old people, built with money given in the past by people of the parish. The Fishmongers' Company also once had magnificent almshouses on the present site of the Metropolitan Tabernacle.

References and further reading

1. *Domesday Book; Surrey*. Text & transl: John Morris, Phillimore, 1975.
2. *Survey* pp 81-2, 91-94, 127-8, plates 49, 53, parish boundaries map.
3. *Victoria County History of Surrey*, 1912, reprint, for University of London, 1967, vol 4, pp 74-77 and other references.

Maps -
4. *Plan of Walworth Manor 1681*. London Topographical Society publ. 1932.
5. John Rocque - *Map of London and 10 miles round*, 1741-1745,
6. John Rocque - *Plan of the Cities of London and Westminster and Borough of Southwark, 1747*, reprinted as *The A-Z of Georgian London*, London Topographical Society, 1982.

For more detailed study -
7. *Archives of St Mary Newington Parish*, including *Vestry Minutes*; *Ratebooks*; *Apprenticeship indentures*, 1675-1847, (some indexes and calenders available); *Removal and Settlement Orders*. See S.C. Humphrey - *A guide to the archives in Southwark Local Studies Library*, S'wark Council, 1992.

3. GEORGIAN AND EARLY VICTORIAN WALWORTH

One group of houses in Walworth is often seen on television. Since 1978, it has been the headquarters of the Labour Party. But the 'Terrace', 140-152 Walworth Road, was not originally intended for that purpose, quite the opposite. These houses, though very much restored, are about 200 years old. The pediment with a medallion was once the centre of a longer terrace.

When they were new, these were the elegant homes of well-to-do people, with servants who slept in the attics and cooked meals in the basement kitchens for the master and mistress 'upstairs'. The 'Terrace' survives from the first stage in Walworth's development, when the area south of the Elephant and Castle began to change from a country village to become, for a time, a high- class suburb of London. New bridges over the Thames and improved roads and transport had made it easier for successful business and professional gentlemen to live out of London, in places like Walworth, and commute daily by carriage or coach to the City or Westminster. Walworth Road, Old Kent Road, New Kent Road, Kennington Park Road, and, indeed, most main roads leading into the capital, were once lined with Georgian houses similar to these, built when George III was king. The east side of Kennington Park Road has survived little changed and gives a good idea of what the other roads must once have looked like. Notice particularly the elegant doorways and fanlights of some of the houses, for example, Nos.95, 101, 125, and 127. They are now part of a Conservation Area, 'an area of special architectural or historic interest, the character or appearance of which it is desirable to preserve or enhance'.

Most of the old houses still standing in Walworth Road and Old Kent Road are rather run-down and hidden behind shops which have been built in what were once their long front gardens. The best way to see them is from the top of a bus. An inscription high up on the front of 252, Old Kent Road, reads 'Surrey Place built 1784', the original name for that group of houses. There is actually one long front garden still to be seen in Walworth Road; rather surprisingly it is in front of the Police Station. Over 200 years ago, Mr Keen, a local landowner, and landlord of the Beehive Tavern, built a terrace of houses, known as Keen's Row, in Walworth Road. For himself he built a larger residence, 'Walworth House', set well back from the road with an extra long garden. Later it became the home of a Dr Carter, who allowed Carter Street to be cut through his land. About 1860 Walworth House became a Police Station. It has been rebuilt but fortunately has kept its garden.

Some of the finest Georgian houses still to be seen in Walworth are in Surrey

Square, just off Old Kent Road. They were built in 1792. Notice especially the pediment above the centre of the terrace, with its beautiful fan-shape decoration in Coade stone. Note also the wrought iron railings, and, at the entrances to Nos. 42 and 50, torch snuffers for residents returning home after dark in the days long before electric or even gas street lighting. Like the houses in Kennington Park Road, these are 'listed buildings', on the Department of the Environment's *List of buildings of special architectural or historic interest*. Surrey Square was never actually a square, just a terrace originally longer, as a third of the houses were demolished when the school was built in 1884. When first built the houses looked out on to a formal garden. The architect of Surrey Square was Michael Searles. 155, Old Kent Road, is by the same architect. This neat, fairly small white house was Searles' own home. 'The Paragon', a crescent-shape development by Searles, used to overlook the crescent-shape garden in New Kent Road, but was demolished when the school was built in, what was named, Searles Road. The word 'paragon' means model of perfection; Searles' other 'Paragon', on Blackheath, is still much admired.

Two hundred years ago, the period when Surrey Square and Walworth's other Georgian houses were being built, must have been a good time for 'property developers' who owned, or bought, land when it was just fields and soon made money turning them into streets of houses. The site of Surrey Square had been one such field, part of a large estate belonging to a farmer, James Brace. Development of the Brace Estate began in 1763 when it was leased to Thomas Clutton, 'a bricklayer'. He did so well from this and other developments that he was able to lease and rebuild the Walworth Manor House, where he lived in style, driving home up Walworth Road in his 'neat post-chaise' drawn by some of his twenty-five horses. On the farmlands still belonging to Manor House he had cows, pigs, geese, ducks and chickens. Older people still remember the Rolls Estate. Until the 1960's it owned many streets in Walworth, Camberwell and Bermondsey, mainly near Old Kent Road and Rolls Road. This estate began about two hundred years ago when John Rolls, 'a cow-keeper', or dairyman, started leasing fields and building on them. Michael Searles was his surveyor and 155 Old Kent Road later became the Rolls Estate Office. Charles Stewart Rolls, great grandson of John Rolls, and his partner, Henry Royce, were the founders of Rolls-Royce Motors.

Street-names to the west of Walworth Road, for example, Penton Place and Chapter Road, are reminders of others involved in the early development of Walworth. From 1686 much of this land had been leased by the Penton family from the Dean and Chapter. In 1774 Henry Penton got permission to let some of his Walworth fields for building. Bricks for the new houses could be made on the spot as he also got permission to dig there for brick clay. 140-152 Walworth Road are some of his houses. The architect was a local man, Francis Hurlblatt, of Church Row, Newington Butts. Most of the other houses on Penton's land have since been replaced by later developments. One of their prosperous residents was Thomas Fish of 13 Penton Row, site of 228 Walworth Road, reputed to have been a millionaire. His son, naturally enough known as the 'Goldfish', kept the house as his London residence until his death in 1861. Penton's name is remembered also in north London, where he was responsible for Pentonville. The Brandon Estate, erected in the 1960's, takes its name from an earlier development, undertaken by Thomas Brandon, a 'gardener' and his brother Samuel, who leased some of the Penton lands for building. Samuel lived in one of the houses in Surrey Square when they were new. A group of streets off Kennington Park Road with rather aristocratic names, De Laune Street, Sharsted Street, Doddington Grove, Faunce Street, and also the Faunce Arms, were built on land that once belonged to the Faunce and De Laune families of Sharsted Court, Doddington, Kent.

A Companion from London to Brighthelmstone (Brighton), published in 1800, gives some idea of the class of people in Walworth about two hundred years ago. It lists many 'academies for young gentlemen' and 'boarding schools for young ladies' in the area. At one of these, the Marlborough House Boarding School, Marlborough Place, Walworth Road, present site of the Pit-Stop Garage, fees for the young ladies were 30 guineas a year, or, for 'parlour boarders', 50 guineas. Extra fees were charged for 'geography and use of globes', drawing, music and dancing. As the prospectus says, health was promoted 'by frequent walking and such other exercises as are consistent with propriety'. The name, 'Rodney House Academy', still appears on the gatepost of 124, New Kent Road. When this Georgian house was new it was a school for young gentlemen.

As time went on, Walworth's population increased and new streets were built off the main roads. Those who only know Walworth for its traffic and its high-rise estates should take a walk through its early Victorian streets and its four Conservation Areas. Two of these pleasant oases, built up about 150 years ago, are to be found west of Walworth Road just beyond the railway viaduct, which in 1860, was built across once peaceful streets. The Sutherland Square Conservation Area stretches from Carter Street to Fielding Street and includes Lorrimore Square and Lorrimore Road. Above some of the houses in this road are their original names, Minerva Terrace 1852, Surrey Terrace, and Sussex Terrace. Look out also for interesting details, the cast-iron railings in Sutherland Square topped with 'palmettes' little palms, or with turrets, and the decorative window-box containers in Fielding Street. South of Sutherland Square is the Grosvenor Park Conservation Area, consisting of Grosvenor Park, Grosvenor Terrace and part of Urlwin Street. These grand houses were restored in the 1970's for Southwark Council tenants. The Kennington Park Road Conservation Area includes, not only the main road, but also Kennington Park Place and St Agnes Place, a charming corner, mostly small houses of the early 1800's with one large mansion, formerly the Bishop's House, now a Children's Day Nursery; designed in 1895 by the famous architect, Norman Shaw. The Octavia Hill Conservation Area, to the east of Walworth Road (see chap.10) includes Peacock Terrace, Liverpool Grove, neat small houses, built in 1842, similar houses in Trafalgar Street, Cadiz Street, Dawes Street and Lytham Street; and also Aylesbury Road, Wooler Street, Brettell Street and part of Villa Street which are a little later.

George Yates, a family firm which did much good building, still has its offices at 205 Walworth Road. Its founder, Edward Yates, built Larcom Street, in 1876, a typical mid-Victorian street, and also Aldbridge Street, Darwin Street and Chatham Street. Houses in these and others of Walworth's Victorian streets, for example, Exon Street, Fremantle Street, and Madron

Street, now restored to look as good as new, and no doubt modernised inside, make attractive homes for families today.

References and further reading

1. R.W.Bowers - *Sketches of Southwark old and new,* Wesley, 1902..
2. Bridget Cherry and Nikolaus Pevsner - *The buildings of England; London 2: South*, Penguin Books, 1983. pp 593-7.
3. Department of the Environment - *List of buildings of special architectural or historic interest; Southwark.*
4. Southwark Council Development Department - *Octavia Hill, Sutherland Square, Grosvenor Park, and Kennington Park Road*, typescript reports.
5. *Survey.* pp 82-84, 88-90.
For more detailed study -
6. W. Bonwitt - *Michael Searles: a Georgian architect and surveyor,* Society of Architectural Historians of Great Britain, 1987.
7. H.J.Dyos - *Exploring the urban past*, C.U.P., 1982. Chap. 11. *A Victorian speculative builder, Edward Yates.*
8. *Papers of the Clutton family of Walworth*, 1789-1809 and 1838, Southwark Deeds 22/1.
9. *The A to Z of Regency London*, Harry Margary,1985.

4. GARDENS, PLEASURE GROUNDS AND A ZOO

Yesterday Mr Groom of Walworth, the celebrated grower of tulips, afforded a private view of his splendid collection, 250,000 of these beautiful flowers. Among the fashionable visitors were Lord Beresford, the Marquis of Westminster, the Duke of Beaufort, the Bishops of Chester and Winchester.

Times 17th May 1836

Residents of Walworth's Georgian houses, when they were new, did not have far to walk to find themselves amongst orchards, nurseries, greenhouses, and flower gardens. Before modern transport and cold storage, Walworth was one of the villages near enough to central London to supply its citizens with fresh produce. Even luxury fruit, which today would be imported, was grown in Walworth. *Parradisus Terrestris*, 'Earthly Paradise', a book published in 1629, praised the 'Newington Peach, ripe about Bartholomewtide', (24th August), A map of 1787 shows a peach garden just north of New Kent Road. In 1789 John Abercrombie of Newington Butts published *The Hothouse Gardener*, a book on growing pineapples, early grapes, peaches and nectarines. The Driver family of Old Kent Road had 40 acres of nursery gardens. Their conservatory, 240 feet long, was about where East Street Library is today, 'Surrey Place' was built on part of their land. James Maddock and Son, of the 'Walworth Garden', on the site of Sutherland Square, published *The Florists' Directory*, with beautiful pictures of the flowers they grew. It was their nursery which was later taken over by Henry Groom, famous for his tulips.

Some of Walworth's gardens were pleasure grounds, places to visit for a day's outing in the summer, easily reached on foot, or by horse and carriage, from the crowded City. The Beehive pub in Carter Street, with an old fashioned beehive as its sign, takes its name from the famous Beehive Tea Gardens. The cricket field at the Beehive was the home ground of the Montpelier Cricket Club until it moved in 1844, to the Oval and became the foundation of the Surrey County Cricket Club. Pelier Street and the small open space called Pelier Garden are on the site of the Montpelier Tavern and Tea Gardens.

1831 was an exciting year for Walworth, especially for children. It saw the opening on Lorrimore Common of Walworth's most famous attraction, its very own zoo, rivalling if not surpassing the London Zoo, opened only three years before in Regent's Park. The proprietor of the 'Royal Surrey Zoological Gardens' was Edward Cross who had moved his menagerie to Walworth from its original home in the Strand. The zoo had lions, tigers, elephants, reindeer and llamas, a pair of dromedaries presented by the ruler of Egypt, and a giant tortoise on which children could ride. Five giraffes, the first ever to be seen by the public in England, were brought from Africa by an Arab boy named Fadlallah. A model of them is in the Cuming Museum. Before the Crystal Palace was thought of, the Walworth zoo had a huge circular glass building, about 100 metres across, with cages in the centre surrounded by a walk for visitors to view the animals. The zoo attracted royal patrons, hence its name. In 1848 Queen Victoria herself, with Prince Albert and the royal children, paid it a visit. They were especially interested in a rather unusual animal friendship, a tigress and a dog who lived in the same cage.

THE GIRAFFES, AND THEIR NUBIAN ATTENDANTS, AT THE SURREY ZOOLOGICAL GARDENS.

Fadlallah feeding the giraffes,1843

An average of 8,000 visitors a day came to see the animals and also the magnificent entertainments which took place at the Surrey Gardens. The lake on Lorrimore Common was used as foreground to huge panoramas.

One of these represented Vesuvius, as seen across the Bay of Naples. In the evening, with a firework display, the volcano seemed to be actually erupting. Another panorama showed the city of Rome, the lake, with boats on it, representing the River Tiber.

> At the Surrey Menagerie everyone knows,
> (Because 'tis a place to which everyone goes)
> There's a model of Rome, and as round it one struts,
> One sinks the remembrance of Newington Butts
> And having a shilling laid down at the portal,
> One fancies one's self in the city immortal.

*The Comic Almanac,*1843

Realistic battle scenes were also presented. With cannon firing, which set the animals roaring, the noise must have been deafening.

The Surrey Gardens were famous also for music. In 1845 a celebrated French conductor, Monsieur Jullien, took over, with an orchestra of up to 400 musicians. In 1856 the zoo closed but on part of the site was built the huge Royal Surrey Gardens Music Hall which could hold 10,000 people for Jullien's high-class concerts. In July, 1857, Jullien's orchestra was joined by eleven military bands and singers from the Royal Italian Opera Company and the Royal Surrey Choral Society, a thousand performers in all, for concerts in aid of Mary Seacole, the heroic and enterprising black woman from Jamaica, who went, on her own initiative, like Florence Nightingale, to nurse the wounded in the Crimean War. The Surrey Gardens Music Hall also attracted crowds on Sundays as it was used by the great preacher, Charles Haddon Spurgeon, before his Metropolitan Tabernacle was built at the Elephant.

Soon, however, Walworth's population increased so much that all its land was wanted for building. In 1872 the Surrey Gardens were sold. The concert hall was demolished and the 13 acres of 'attractive pleasure grounds laid out with great taste, adorned with statuary and fountains – and a magnificent lake,' disappeared beneath closely packed streets, Sturgeon Road, Pasley Road, Marsland Road, Manor Place, Danson Road, and Borrett Road. All that is left as a reminder of the past are pub names, the Giraffe, Penton Place, and the Surrey Gardens Arms, Chapter Road, and because of Spurgeon's preaching, The Surrey Gardens Memorial Hall. And as a reminder of Walworth's earlier flower, fruit and vegetable growers? Perhaps the Walworth Garden Farm, set up in 1987, in Braganza Street, will give young people a chance to revive something of that old tradition.

References and further reading

1. Richard Altick - *Shows of London*, Harvard University Press, 1978.
2. R.W. Bowers - *Sketches of Southwark old and new*, pp406-10.
3. David Lemmon - *The official history of the Surrey County Cricket Club*, Christopher Helm, 1989, chap: 2.
4. H.H. Montgomery - *History of Kennington*, Stacey Gold,1889. pp 169-76.
5. *Survey*. pp 86-89 and 406-10.

For more detailed study -

6. Jim Gould - *James Maddock, the Walworth Garden and the Florist's Directory*, Garden History, 1991.
7. J.H.Harvey - *The nurseries on Milne's land-use map*, L.M.A.S.,1973.
8. Caroline Lucas - *The Royal Surrey Zoological Gardens*, typescript, 1991.
9. Playbills for Surrey Gardens etc.

5. THE CUMINGS AND THEIR MUSEUM

Where in Walworth can you find a wooden figure, over 3000 years old, of the ancient Egyptian god, Osiris, a whalebone bracelet brought home by Captain Cook from Alaska, a model of Newington Butts before 1850, Roman sculptures found beneath Southwark Cathedral, and such an oddity as a cap decorated with human teeth worn by a 19th century dentist? These are, just a few of the thousands of objects in Walworth's own treasure house, the Cuming Museum, which has the finest collection of London's local museums, a collection built up by a truly remarkable Walworth family.

It began over 200 years ago at '3 Dean's Row', 196 Walworth Road, present site of MacDonald's, but site then of a Georgian house, home of young

Many visitors are drawn to the Cuming Museum's wonderful collections

Richard Cuming. The Cumings were one of the well-to-do families living in Walworth at that time. For his fifth birthday on 20th March 1782, Richard was given some fossils and an old coin by a neighbour, Mrs Coleman, of Manor Place. This started him on a lifetime of collecting. When he was fourteen he made the tiny cardboard cabinet for his collection which is still to be seen in the Cuming Museum. Richard grew up to be a man of wide learning, interested especially in scientific research. When Michael Faraday was still a child, Richard Cuming was making a microscope, a magic lantern, and an 'electrifying machine', all still in the Museum. His friends included artists such as Turner, and scholars, such as his neighbour, Thomas Taylor of Manor Place, known as 'the Platonist', whose study of the ancient Greek philosopher, earned him an entry in the *Dictionary of National Biography*.

But when England was at war with Napoleon, Richard Cuming was also ready to defend his country. At 21 he enlisted in the Newington Volunteers.

As a subaltern he wore a helmet with a plume, red jacket with black edging and brass buttons, and white trousers. His sword and badge are in the Cuming Museum. Fortunately, however, Napoleon did not invade England, and Richard could devote most of his long life to building up his immense private museum. He lived at a particularly exciting time for collectors. Explorers were opening up the whole world and archaeologists were excavating ancient sites such as Pompeii and finding out about ancient peoples such as the Etruscans and the Egyptians. It was an age of great collectors and of the first museums in London, two of which were in the present London Borough of Southwark, the Leverian in Blackfriars Road, and the Surrey Museum, Marlborough Place, Walworth Road. Richard Cuming bought items from both of these when they were sold up. From the Leverian came objects from Cook's voyages and also such curiosities as a stuffed dancing bear and a monkey, dressed as a scribe, with notebook in hand, to take the names of visitors. Both are still in the Museum.

In later life Richard lived at 63 Kennington Park Road, where, after his death in 1870, his son, Henry Syer Cuming, continued to live, and carried on his father's work. Both father and son carefully researched objects added to the collection and labelled them in their neat, small handwriting. Henry Syer, also a scholar, became Vice-President of the British Archaeological Association. His very wide interests are shown in his writings. There are articles by him on about 200 different subjects, ranging from King Alfred to mermaids, from Roman pottery to Easter eggs. He never married, but lived with his sister, Ann, herself an artist and poet.

In 1902, when Henry Syer Cuming died, he left all his collections and library to the Borough of Southwark, together with investments for a museum in which they could be on show to the public. The Cuming Museum, in the same building as Newington Library, 155 Walworth Road, opened in 1906. In the 1930's it was advertised on the trams as 'the British Museum in miniature'. Closed in 1941 due to war damage it was reopened in 1959. In 1992 it won a National Heritage Museum of the Year Award.

The Cumings had a special interest in the history of London and their native

Southwark area. They lived at a time of redevelopment, when a collector with a seeing eye could acquire items which would otherwise have been lost for ever. Since the war, the Cuming has specialised in the history and archaeology of Southwark, adding to the Cuming's own collections, with more recent finds and local bygones. The main permanent display cases show Southwark through the ages, from the Romans to the present day.

As well as objects, the Cuming family left an enormous collection of papers. In fact they seem never to have thrown anything away! These papers are very valuable for Southwark history. They include tradesmen's advertisements picturing local shops, and handbills telling what was on at local theatres. Richard Cuming's brother, John Brompton Cuming, was an artist who exhibited at the Royal Academy. Beautiful water-colour paintings by him, and others of the family, done long before the invention of photography, provide a pictorial record of the old villages of Walworth, Camberwell and Peckham.

References and further reading
1. R.W.Bowers - *Sketches of Southwark old and new*, pp 575-590
2. Richard W Mould - *Southwark men of mark*, Bowers, 1905, pp 61-64.

6. SOME WALWORTH NOTABLES

Michael Faraday
It is impossible to think of today's world without the discoveries or inventions of two famous scientists born in Walworth two hundred years ago, Michael Faraday and Charles Babbage. The whole world knows about Faraday, whose discovery of electromagnetic induction, the production of electric currents by means of magnetism, made possible all the modern use of electricity. Though the family left the neighbourhood when he was a small boy, local people have always been proud to remember that, in 1791, Newington Butts was his birthplace. The Cuming Museum has the Faraday family Bible in which Michael's father wrote the dates of birth of Michael and his brothers and sisters, also an early electric dynamo used by Faraday.

A Michael Faraday Memorial Library, set up in Southwark in 1927, is now housed in the Local Studies Library. When the Michael Faraday School, Portland Street, was first opened in 1897, the Royal Institution presented it with a bust of Faraday, 'as an incentive to Newingtonians yet unborn to lift themselves out of their sordid surroundings even as Faraday himself did'. The school, rebuilt in 1978, joined in the nationwide celebrations which marked the Faraday Bicentenary in 1991.

Charles Babbage

Charles Babbage (1791-1871)
Mathematician, Astronomer, and Computer Pioneer
was born near this site.
Plaque on Southwark Council offices,Larcom Street

Charles Babbage, the other Walworth notable born in 1791, 'father of the modern computer', was a man so far in advance of his time that he was almost forgotten for many years, but now at last, has come into his own. He invented calculating machines, called by him an 'analytical engine' and a 'differential engine', which were the foundation of one of the greatest achievements of 20th century technology. Parts of both his machines have been set up in the Science Museum. What Babbage really lacked to make his inventions work was Faraday's discovery, the power of electricity. Like Faraday, Babbage moved away from Walworth when quite young. He did recall, in his autobiography, being taken by his nurse to the Montpelier Gardens.

Mary Wollstonecraft

Walworth is also proud to be associated with a remarkable woman pioneer, Mary Wollstonecraft. Her ideas on women's rights anticipate by 200 years those of today's women's movement. During her formative years she spent much time with her friend Fanny Blood, who lived in Newington Butts, and also stayed for a time with 'Taylor the Platonist' at his home in Manor Place. A Southwark council plaque has been erected on the Southwark College building in Blackfriars Road, at the corner of Dolben Street, (formerly George Street), where Mary had lodgings shortly before the publication of her book, *A vindication of the rights of woman*, in 1792.

Robert Browning

Two of England's greatest writers, Robert Browning the poet, probably best remembered as the author of *The Pied Piper of Hamelin*; and John Ruskin, author, artist and thinker, both knew Walworth as children, coming regularly to church here. Browning Street and Robert Browning School, John Ruskin Street and John Ruskin School are named after them. Browning's parents had met when they were both Sunday School teachers at the York Street Chapel, an Independent Church, just off Walworth Road, erected in 1790. In 1812, when their son Robert, the future poet, was born, they brought him from their home in Southampton Way, North Camberwell, to be christened at the Chapel. As a boy he attended the Chapel with his parents and sister, Sarianna, sitting in the gallery overlooking the pulpit, listening (or, it is said, sometimes not listening!) to the sermons of the Rev. George Clayton, a minister of great reputation, who was at York Street for fifty years. Much later Browning had become so famous that York Street was renamed Browning Street, and the York Street Chapel became Browning Hall. The Robert Browning Settlement (see chapter 10) was set up here in 1895, as a 'World Memorial to the Great Poet'. Browning Hall was finally destroyed by fire in 1978, but the Settlement still treasures in its museum over a hundred items associated with Robert Browning, including a bust by his son Robert Barrett Browning, portraits, letters, the Register of Baptisms with entries for Robert and Sarianna, the font where they were christened, and the family pew from the old Chapel.

John Ruskin

Young John Ruskin, born 1819, was brought by his parents to another Independent church in Walworth, the Beresford Street Chapel. They came on Sundays from their home on Herne Hill to hear its famous preacher, Dr Andrews. When he was old, Ruskin well remembered the Chapel, with its 'pews, well shut in, by – neatly brass-latched deal doors; and the 'pulpit, – high as the level of the front galleries, and decorated with a cushion of crimson velvet, – with gold tassels at the corners; when I was tired of the sermon, I liked watching the bright colour of the folds and creases when the clergyman thumped it.' Beresford Street was renamed John Ruskin Street, but the old Chapel only just survives as a car warehouse. Ruskin had other associations with Walworth. Until he was 15 he did not go regularly to school but was taught by tutors from the 'academies' of what he called 'tutorial Walworth'. Dr Andrews taught him Greek and Latin, and Mr Rowbotham of 'Rowbotham's Classical, Mathematical and Commercial Academy', Walworth Road, near the Elephant and Castle, walked out to Herne Hill, two evenings a week, to teach him mathematics and French. Some books used by Ruskin as a schoolboy are in the Ruskin Collection at the Local Studies Library, and also text-books on French, German, and algebra by Dr Rowbotham.

George Tinworth

The remarkable potter, George Tinworth, was a real local boy, born in 1843 and brought up in the crowded back streets of later 19th century Walworth, Milk Street and later Hope Street, alleys to the west of Walworth Road, now demolished. George's father was a wheelwright, making wheels, probably for market barrows. Young George had little education. He was supposed to help his father, but at heart he was always an artist. He really liked to spend his time in the workshop carving figures from spare bits of wood or stone. He used to get another boy to watch out for his father's return when he was doing this! Later he pawned his overcoat to pay the fees for evening classes at the Lambeth School of Art, where he became friendly with some other young men from Walworth, Robert Martin and his three brothers, who were to become noted for their 'Martinware' pottery. At 21, Tinworth won a place at the Royal Academy Schools. He spent his working life at Doulton's, the great pottery making firm, which was then in Lambeth. His parents, were members of the York Street Chapel, and he knew the Bible stories well from reading them with his mother when he was a child. At Doulton's, he became especially famous for modelling Bible scenes, which were admired by Ruskin and other visitors to Royal Academy exhibitions. The Cuming Museum has two of these lifelike pottery reliefs in which the figures stand out like characters on a stage. One shows *The mocking of Christ*, by the soldiers before the Crucifixion. The other, a scene from the Old Testament, *The Jews making bricks in Egypt*, was given to the Museum by

Doulton's as a Tinworth memorial. The Museum also has Tinworth's model for a Shakespeare memorial and several small pottery figure groups, such as the lively *Children on a cart*, looking just as he might have seen them in the back streets of Walworth.

Samuel Palmer
Samuel Palmer, the landscape artist, was also born in Walworth. His birthplace, in 1805, was in one of Walworth's Georgian houses, 42 Surrey Square, now marked with a plaque.

Elizabeth Siddall
Elizabeth Siddall, born in 1834 in Old Kent Road, also became an artist and the beautiful model and wife of Dante Gabriel Rossetti, the famous Pre-Raphaelite painter.

References and further reading
1. Richard W Mould - *Southwark men of mark*, Bowers, 1905
2. Brian Bowers - *Michael Faraday and the modern world*, E.P.A. Press,1991
3. L. Pearce Williams - *Michael Faraday*, Chapman and Hall, 1965
4. Anthony Hyman - *Charles Babbage; pioneer of the computer*, O.U.P., 1982
5. D Swade - *Charles Babbage and his calculating engines*, Science Museum, 1991
6. Maria Calcraft - *Robert Browning's London*, Browning Society 1989
7. James S Dearden - *John Ruskin's Camberwell*, Brentham Press, 1990
8. Claire Tomalin - *Life and death of Mary Wollstonecraft*, 2nd ed., Penguin, 1992
9. Peter Rose - *George Tinworth*, C.D.N.Corporation,U.S.A., 1982
10. George Tinworth - *Autobiography*, unpublished manuscript.

7.   OLD KENT ROAD AND THE ELEPHANT AND CASTLE

Centuries ago, even when the Old Kent Road was little more than a track between fields, it was always one of the great highways of England. Packhorses and heavy carts laden with goods, and herds of cattle, driven on foot, made their way slowly to the markets of London. The signs of pubs on the Old Kent Road, the Dun Cow and the Kentish Drovers, are a reminder of those days. In the Middle Ages pilgrims to the shrine of St Thomas à Becket at Canterbury came this way. In the *Prologue to the Canterbury Tales*, Chaucer tells how they set out from the Tabard Inn, which was in Borough High Street. Their first halt, was at the stream which marked the boundary between Walworth and Camberwell. The place became known as St Thomas à Watering, the present site of the Thomas à Becket pub. Occasionally, there was a royal procession along Old Kent Road, or 'Kinges Street'. When Henry V and his army came back victorious from the Battle of Agincourt, in 1415, they marched from the coast, through Kent, and at Blackheath were joined by the Mayor of London, the aldermen in their red robes and four hundred citizens on horseback. At St Thomas à Watering these were joined by the clergy of London and the great procession continued up 'Kinges Street', and over Old London Bridge to the City. Some sights on Old Kent Road were not so pleasant. Travellers in days gone by passed a gallows set up at St Thomas à Watering, where criminals and traitors were hung. Near where the Flyover is today was the Lock Hospital for Lepers, built here away from the City, as people feared to catch this dread disease. The poor lepers carried a bell round their necks to let people know they were walking in the Locks Fields near their hospital, fields which are now covered by the Heygate Estate.

Even in early times the Elephant and Castle was a traffic junction, as here old roads from the south, Walworth Road, and what is now Kennington Park Road, and from the west, Lambeth Road, joined the road to London Bridge and the City. By the time travellers reached this point some must have come a long way, perhaps even from the Sussex coast. No wonder that, in 1641 John Flaxman, a blacksmith, set up his forge to shoe their horses, on an island site between the roads. It became known as the White Horse and is shown on the 1681 map, with a sign hanging outside. Blacksmiths must always have been in demand at the Elephant and Castle when all traffic was horse-drawn. Michael Faraday's father was a blacksmith. The old St Mary Newington church had a memorial to another blacksmith, James Blackburn, who died in 1811 –

My sledge and hammer lie declined,
My bellows too have lost their wind
My fire's extinct, my forge decayed
And in the dust my vice is laid,
My coal is spent, my iron gone,
My nails are drove, my work is done
My fire dried corpse here lies at rest
My soul, smoke like, soars to be blest.

No doubt travellers to and from London also stopped for something to eat and drink. The smithy became an inn, its sign an elephant with a 'castle', on its back, the Elephant and Castle. Probably the 'castle' was really a 'houdah', a grand seat, such as eastern rulers used. The first reference to the name, is in the *Court Leet Book of the Manor of Walworth*. On March 21st 1765, the Court met 'at the Elephant and Castle, Newington'. The inn was able to provide a good 'Bill of Fare' after the meeting. Previously the Court had met at other inns in Newington Causeway, for example, the Ship, or at the Walworth Manor House. It is not known why the name Elephant and Castle was chosen for this particular inn but it was not an uncommon sign. An Elephant and Castle appears, for example, on a 17th century trade token from Tooley Street, Bermondsey. An Elephant and Castle is the sign of the Cutlers' Company, who probably chose it because ivory from elephants' tusks was used for knife handles.

In the great days of coaching both the Elephant and Castle area and the Old Kent Road got more and more busy. In the 18th and early 19th centuries new bridges were built over the Thames, Westminster, Blackfriars, Vauxhall, Waterloo and Southwark bridges. Roads leading to all the bridges radiated from the Elephant and Castle; in the words of Charles Dickens, 'that ganglion of roads from Kent and Surrey and of streets from the bridges of London centring in the far-famed Elephant'. Coaches to many parts of southern England called regularly at the Elephant and Castle to pick up passengers, and old pictures show that traffic jams there were nearly as bad as at the present day! The inn became so well-known that it gave its name to the whole surrounding area. The pick-up point for coaches on the Old

Kent Road was another famous inn, the Bricklayers' Arms, on the present site of the Flyover.

The new roads were built, and old roads improved, by Turnpike Trusts, groups of people who took over a stretch of road and undertook to keep it in good repair. In 1751, one Turnpike Trust built the 'New' Kent Road, from Old Kent Road to the Elephant and Castle. This was when the Kent Road became the 'Old' Kent Road. To get money to build and repair roads the Turnpike Trusts were allowed to set up tollgates and collect tolls off the coaches, carriages, wagons and people on horseback who used them. There were two tollgates where the Flyover is today, across New Kent Road, and across Great Dover Street, and another across Old Kent Road, between the Dun Cow and the Green Man. The Newington Tollgate was in Newington Causeway, just north of the Elephant and Castle. The Gateway Estate marks the site of the Camberwell Gate in Walworth Road. Tollgates throughout London were abolished by Act of Parliament in 1865. The old Newington Tollgate has been set up at the back of the Livesey Museum, Old Kent Road and the Cuming Museum has tollgate tickets and portraits of the tollgate keepers.

Today the words, 'Elephant and Castle' mean not just a road junction but a bus stop, an underground, and a rail station. In the past there was very little public transport, for ordinary Londoners. Not many could afford, or find a place on the few short distance coaches which clattered down Walworth Road from the City and Westminster to Camberwell. For most people without their own carriage there was only 'shank's pony', their own two feet. The first real improvement was the horse-bus. Buses were introduced to London in 1829 and by 1833 over one hundred were licensed to travel, via the Elephant and Castle, down Walworth Road. A two-horse double-decker, with seating for 24 passengers, in use in 1875, on the No.12 bus-route from Peckham to Oxford Circus, is on show in the London Transport Museum. It was one of Thomas Tilling's buses, the company founded in Peckham. The Cuming Museum has a model of a four-horse bus used on the same route in 1900. The change to motor buses began in 1904.

By then, instead of taking a bus at the Elephant, or in Old Kent Road, you could also hop on a tram. In 1871 workmen had laid tramlines down the main roads for horse trams, mostly two decker, drawn by two horses. The lines made it easier for horses to pull heavy loads, so fares came down. In 1903 'horse-power' was replaced by the London County Council electric trams. Trams carried crowds of people very cheaply to their daily work. But tramlines could be dangerous if cyclists caught their wheels or pedestrians their shoes in them. Din and congestion reached a peak at the Elephant, where trams came from all directions, in the midst of other traffic, and tramlines were laid so close together that it was impossible for two trams to pass side by side. By 1911 subways had to be built for pedestrians to cross the roads. In spite of their drawbacks, however, many people loved the trams, and turned out sadly to say goodbye when, in 1952, trams were abolished throughout London, and the last No.36 made its way down Old Kent Road.

The railway arrived at the Elephant and Castle in 1862. On the 6th October, the Elephant and Castle Station opened and steam engines came roaring over the bridge across Walworth Road, high above the horse-drawn traffic below. In those days there were many railway companies. The Elephant and Castle was served by the London, Chatham and Dover Railway. The line, via Herne Hill, Camberwell, and Walworth, to Blackfriars and Holborn was build high up on arches, a huge undertaking employing hundreds of bricklayers. From the window of a tall flat you may see it, running parallel to Walworth Road, carried on arches above the streets, such as Manor Place, Penrose Street, John Ruskin Street and Grosvenor Terrace. From its early years the railway was popular with working people. It was much quicker than horse-drawn transport and could be very cheap, as there were special 'workmen's tickets' at only a penny each way, for those travelling to work before 7.00a.m. and returning after 6.00p.m. People worked long hours in those days. In addition to the Elephant and Castle Station, in Elephant Road, there were once two other stations on the line, both of which closed in 1916. Station Road, off Camberwell New Road, was the site of one of them. The Station Tavern in John Ruskin Street, is a reminder of the other, known as Camberwell Gate, or Walworth Road Station. Mornings and

A horsebus arrives at the Elephant and Castle

evenings this station was very busy, both with people getting on here to travel in to the City, and with people getting off, to work at the factories and warehouses that lined the nearby Grand Surrey Canal, on the site of Burgess Park. The narrow stairs leading down to the street were so crammed at rush hours they became known as the 'Walworth Shoot'.

On November 4th 1890, the 'tube', a totally new type of railway, came to the Elephant and Castle. Now part of the Northern Line, it was originally called the City and South London Railway, and ran from Stockwell to King William Street. The Prince of Wales, the future King Edward VII, was on board the first train, for this was the first ever electric tube railway in the world, a pioneer for many others to follow. Since 1863 London had had a few underground trains but these were only just below the surface and used smoky steam engines. Before the C.S.L. no trains of any kind had been powered by electricity. The very deep tunnels constructed to take the new 'tube railway' are an engineering feat scarcely realised by the thousands of commuters who go by Underground today – except perhaps if the lifts break down at the Elephant and Castle and they have to toil up the stairs from 16 metres below ground level! Kennington, one of the stations on the line, still has its original station building of 1890. The dome once housed the top of a hydraulic lift. In its early years the fare on this wonderful railway was only twopence all the way; the 'Twopenny Tube'. In 1906 another Underground line reached the Elephant and Castle, the Baker Street and Waterloo Railway, which people called the Bakerloo. It also has its original station, faced with red glazed terracotta, like others of that date.

References and further reading

1. W. H. Blanch - *The Parish of Camberwell*, 1875. pp343-5.
2. *Charles Dickens and Southwark*, L. B. Southwark, 1980.
3. Mark Searle - *Turnpikes and tollbars*, Hutchinson.
4. *Survey.* pp46-8, frontis:, and plates 50a, 74a, 91a.
5. *Walworth in Print*, 1978-88, no.23.
   This publication had many good local history articles.
6. Theo Barker - *Moving millions; a pictorial history of London Transport*, L. T. Museum, 1990.
7. Prinz P. Holman - *The amazing electric tube*, London Transport Museum, 1990.
8. M.A.C. Horne - *The Bakerloo Line*, Nebulous Books,1990.
9. C. F. Dendy Marshall - *A history of the Southern Railway*, revised edition: Ian Allen, 1963

8. CROWDED STREETS

In a turning off the Elephant and Castle, in Newington Butts, in 1900, lived the Hall family, in one room of a large house, mother, father and three children. It was all that could be afforded on the father's wage as a horse-bus conductor.- In this one room they slept, cooked by fire, cleaned from water collected from a cold tap on the landing.

A S Hall - *Home at the beginning of the century*

In 1801, the year of the first census, there were 14,847 people living in the Parish of St Mary Newington. Anyone born that year, who reached the age of eighty, would have seen the neighbourhood completely changed in their lifetime. By 1881 the population had reached 107,850. By 1901 the figure had risen to 122,172, about four times that of 1981. Old maps show the whole area covered with a maze of narrow streets with almost no open space.

How had Walworth changed from a residential neighbourhood with pleasure gardens to such a crowded part of the inner city? Well, the population of London had increased enormously in that period. In addition, factories, warehouses and railways had replaced much housing in the centre so London's population overflowed, engulfing old villages such as Walworth. As the neighbourhood became built up, so the class of residents changed. Most of the well-off people moved out to less crowded places. Their big houses were let off in rooms to poorer people. On the main roads shops replaced front gardens. The population now was working class or very poor. The children had nowhere to play but the streets.

In the back streets and courtyards, some nothing more than slums, many people lived in small four-room houses, two up and two down, with a scullery or wash-house extension at the back, which probably had the only water tap for the whole house. These houses had been built for one family, but though families were large then, they often had to take lodgers in the upstairs rooms to make ends meet. Halpin Place, off East Street gives some idea of that older Walworth; though the houses are well done up now, not over-crowded, quiet and pleasant. John Bennett, author of *I was a Walworth boy*, who was born in 1902, recalled his childhood in one of the bigger houses in East Street, which had three storeys.

'My family occupied the ground floor and one room above. –The children's bedroom was upstairs and there were five of us. The remainder of the house was let by my parents. In the middle were a couple with the wife's mother; the two women made ties and the clatter of their treadle sewing-machine was the only music I had to lull me to sleep. The top floor was occupied by another couple. The husband used to boil winkles on the landing gas-stove on Sunday mornings to sell at a nearby pub.'

Late Victorian Walworth, also had some very different type of housing, great blocks of flats, as close together as possible, put up about the 1880's and 90's, in order to house even more people on the same patch of land. The Surrey Gardens Estate was built up in this way with narrow tunnel-like streets, completely lined with five storey blocks. Only in the 1980's were these replaced with the houses and gardens of Marsland Close and the Pasley Estate. Much still remains of the Pullens Estate to the north of Manor Place. This was a wholesale redevelopment carried out about a hundred years ago by James Pullen and Son, builders, of 73 Penton Place. The flats are well built with large rooms, and with the kind of decoration on the outside that the Victorians loved, even for the dwellings of the poor, but again they were in long terraces, right up to the pavements of narrow streets. No open space, and little room for a through current of air in a hot summer. The estate has now been opened out. Only 360 of the original 650 flats remain. The north side of Thrush Street, has gone, making room for a small park, Pullen's gardens, and the south side has new housing. Amelia Street, Peacock Street, Iliffe Street and Crampton Street look quite different now only one side of each street remains. The flats were once crowded with large families of children; for single people or couples they now make valued homes.

Some Victorian flats are quite grand looking, for example, Darwin Court, Barlow Street, built by the Industrial Dwellings Company in 1881. Probably the best flats were those owned by the Peabody Trust which still has estates in East Street, Larcom Street, and Old Kent Road. The founder of the Trust, George Peabody, was an American who had risen from poor boy to millionaire. Visiting England on business, he saw the conditions in London's slums, and in 1862 gave £500,000, a very large sum in those days, to provide better housing for working class people. Peabody flats each had what was a real luxury in those days, their own kitchen and tap and each block had bathrooms and a laundry room. Modernised now, they still provide good housing for rent. A life-size figure of George Peabody rightly sits in the heart of London, in Threadneedle Street. The well-cared for Guinness Estate in Kennington Park Road was built by a similar Trust, founded by the firm famous for its stout. Refurbishment of St George's Buildings, near the Elephant and Castle, erected in 1900, recently won the building industry's supreme award for quality. But many Victorian flats were not like these. They were really bad. In Blendon Row, off East Street, for example, there were 'tenement blocks' where up to five flats shared a single tap. In the 1930's Southwark Council began a programme of clearing such slums. The brick-built five-storey blocks in Doddington Grove were some of the first of the Council flats.

The crowded streets of Victorian Walworth were not only home, but also a place of work, for many local people. There were no large factories, but many small workshops tucked away in the backyards of houses. There was once a wadding factory in Wadding Street and rope was made from hemp in Hemp Walk. Pain's Fireworks were once made in Walworth Road. Older people may recall the scent from 8, Colworth Grove, off Browning Street, a small house, with machinery set up in what should have been the front parlour. It was the workshop of John Wilde, where 'edge runners', mill-stones set on edge, ground plants into powder for medicines. In its early days the famous 'Keatings' flea powder was a profitable product of this firm! Pullens Estate has one special feature. Yards with workshops, Iliffe Yard, Peacock Yard, etc., were built as part of the whole scheme, so families could not only live but work on the premises. These workshops, just right for craftsmen, are still in demand. Southwark Council's Newington Industrial Estate in Crampton Street, is a new provision for local employment.

For those people in Walworth who could not get work, for the old and sick who were unable to work, for the poorest of the poor, there was only the huge grim institution in Westmoreland Road, Newington Workhouse. In the 1880's over a thousand 'paupers', as they were called, were reduced to living here. In 1896, Charlie Chaplin, age seven, and his elder brother

Sydney, were here for a short time until transferred to special 'Poor Law Residential Schools', for workhouse children, at Hanworth, near Twickenham. Other poor people, who still managed to live in their own homes, had to queue at the workhouse, or 'bunhouse', as they called it, for 'outrelief', a dole of bread, sugar, tea, etc. In its last years, the workhouse buildings, used then only for old people and homeless families, was renamed Newington Lodge. It was demolished in 1969.

Hot potato seller, Tisdall Place,1895

References and further reading

1. H. J. Bennett - *I was a Walworth boy*, Peckham Publishing Project 1980.
2. Walter Besant - *London South of the Thames*, Black 1912. p123.
3. L. J. Carter - *Walworth 1929-1939*, L J Carter Services,1985.
4. A S Hall - *Home at the beginning of the century.* Wally Horwood - *A Walworth boy; looking back on growing up*, 1922-1939.

Two unpublished memoirs in the Local Studies Library.

5. E. J. Orford, ed. - *The book of Walworth*, chaps., 8, 9, 17.

For more detailed study-

6. I. T. Barclay and E. E. Perry - *Report on and survey of housing conditions in the Metropolitan Borough of Southwark*, Weardale Press, 1929. Also many items on individual estates and on Council housing.

7. Brenda Innes - *Edge runners in Walworth*, in London Industrial Archaeology, no.3, G L I A S, 1984.

8. B . G. Morley - *A history of Newington Lodge*, 1849-1969, typescript.

9. *Census returns*, 1841-1881, on microfilms. These list all residents, with their occupations, at each address.

Maps in print include-

10. *The A to Z of Victorian London*, London Topographical Society, 1987. A reprint of G W Bacon - *New large-scale ordnance atlas of London & suburbs*, 1888.

11. *Old Ordnance Survey maps: Old Kent Road*, 1894 and 1914; *Kennington & Walworth*, 1914; The Godfrey edition, publ. by Alan Godfrey.

9. CHURCHES AND SCHOOLS

Just off Walworth Road, facing you at the end of a side turning, is Walworth's oldest building and probably its most beautiful, St Peter's Church, Liverpool Grove. It was designed by the greatest architect of his day and one of the greatest of all English architects, Sir John Soane. Other buildings by him include parts of the Bank of England and Dulwich Picture Gallery. St Peter's was built in 1825, when Walworth was developing as an elegant Georgian suburb, and there was not room for everyone in the old Parish Church of St Mary Newington. It was one of the churches erected in new districts, with the support of the Commissioners for Building New Churches, which had been set up after the Battle of Waterloo ended the long wars with Napoleon. Others not far away included Holy Trinity, Trinity Church Square, also in the old St Mary Newington parish, and St Georges, Wells Way, Camberwell. Like other 'Waterloo churches', St Peter's is in the style of an ancient Greek temple, with columns before the entrance, but it also has an unusual tower which stands out above the rooftops of the small streets around and makes a landmark looking down from the tall blocks of the Aylesbury Estate. The white marble font, where babies have been christened since 1839, was made by Garland and Fieldwick, a local firm of masons. Their former workshop, at 186 Camberwell Road, still has three Coade stone medallions above the entrance. After terrible damage in World War II, St Peter's was well restored and adapted for Christian worship today. Go inside and you find yourself in a haven of peace, light and space.

As Walworth's population increased many more churches were built. One was St John's, Larcom Street. Its architect was Henry Jarvis of Trinity Church Square who designed many other local churches, all in the Gothic style of the Middle Ages which was by then in fashion for church buildings. St John's tower was taken down a few years ago, but it still looks rather like an old village church, tucked away in the heart of a parish it has served well since 1860. St Matthew's, New Kent Road, built 1857, is also by Jarvis. The first St Paul's, Lorrimore Square, built in 1856, about the same time as the older houses around it, was destroyed in World War II. The modern St Paul's is a striking looking building of 1960, the same period as the nearby Brandon Estate. St Agnes Church, St Agnes Place, founded in 1874, was also rebuilt after the war.

Before there was any 'welfare state', social services, NHS, or DSS, the churches were especially concerned about the plight of poor people in Walworth, and, putting Christian faith into action, pioneered ways of improving their lot. *Walworth past and present*, a booklet published in the 1890's, describes the good work being done at St John's, Larcom Street, under its energetic vicar, Arthur Jephson, 'There are country homes for poor children, a day nursery, where infants are well cared for in the absence of their parents, and a registry for the unemployed, which has been the means of getting many a man, in want, the opportunity of earning a living.' To make sure all couples in his parish were properly married, Jephson provided 'penny weddings'. On Easter Sunday, 1901, no less than forty couples were married at one service! The Rev. John W Horsley of St Peter's

St Peter's, Walworth, 1826

was another outstanding vicar. When he saw that children at his church school sometimes fainted with hunger he got the church crypt cleared of coffins and used the space for an early 'school meals service'. He obviously loved children. His vicarage garden became known as the 'Monkey Park' when he set up a small zoo so that, as he said, 'children can come closer to God's creation'. Meeting new needs, the crypt today is a lively social centre. St Paul's Lorrimore Square, which in 1863, held the first Harvest Festival Service in London, had such big congregations it had to open three 'mission churches'. One of them was St Albans, now a Southwark Council Day Centre for the elderly. The foundation stone 'laid by the Lord Bishop of Rochester, August 21st, 1883'; may be seen in Penton Place. The Cross Swords Youth Centre is one of many organisations to be found at the present day St Paul's.

At the Elephant and Castle one building stands out as quite unlike the Shopping Centre, the office blocks and flats. It is the Metropolitan Tabernacle, a big church with a different style of worship from those just described. It has sometimes been called 'the Cathedral of the South London Baptists', but is known to most people as 'Spurgeon's Tabernacle', after the great preacher, Charles Haddon Spurgeon, for whom the church was built in 1861. In those days it could hold 6,000 people, 3,500 sitting and the rest standing, and it was often packed. The facade, with its six giant Corinthian columns still looks as it did in Spurgeon's day, but the church was rebuilt, after World War II, and behind the columns is a modern building. The Crossway Central Mission, on the Heygate Estate, also replaces an older church, demolished about 1970 for road widening.

Walworth has two large Roman Catholic churches, St Wilfred's, Lorrimore Road, built 1915, and English Martyrs, Rodney Road, 1902. This church is dedicated to those who died for their faith in the 16th century, several of them, on the gallows at St Thomas à Watering, after suffering in the prisons of Borough High Street.

East Street, for most people, means market rather than church, but hidden away here are two churches with no grand buildings which have long been

Metropolitan Tabernacle, 1861

centres of Christian worship and service in Walworth's back streets. A plaque high up on the outside rear wall of East Street Baptist Church reads, 'Richmond Street Mission and Schools, established 1859, erected 1875'. (Richmond Street is now Blackwood Street). The foundation stone of the church building facing East Street reads, 'This stone was laid on behalf of HRH Princess Christian, May 8th 1896'. (The Princess was a daughter of Queen Victoria). The founder of the Mission, now the Baptist Church, was John Dunn, a follower of Spurgeon.

The other East Street church is St Christopher's, the church of the Pembroke College Mission. A hundred years ago there was a wide gap between the wealthy young men who went to Oxford or Cambridge University and people living in the poorer parts of London. Some students felt it was their Christian duty to bridge that gap by living with and helping those less fortunate than themselves. In 1886, Pembroke College, Cambridge, opened the Pembroke College Mission in Tatum Street, Walworth. The hall was built in 1892 and the church above it completed in 1909. All kinds of clubs and sports for young people, went on here. The good work of Pembroke continues today and also its close links with Cambridge.

Walworth Road Methodist Church, is better known to most local people as 'Clubland'. Under the remarkable Jimmie Butterworth, minister here from 1922-76, these buildings housed one of the biggest and most famous youth clubs in the country. The letters LS on the outside stand for its ideals, 'Loyalty and Service'. FCC means Federation of Christian Clubs. The spacious buildings, for church, gym, library, theatre, etc. and also hostel, were erected thanks to Butterworth's enthusiastic money-raising. In the USA he enlisted the support of celebrities such as Bob Hope, the comedian, and, in this country, of Freddie Mills the boxer. Clubland, first completed just before the outbreak of war, was destroyed two years later, but Butterworth never despaired, and raised money, for the present building, which was opened by the Queen-Mother in 1964. The church was designed by Edward Maufe, architect of Guildford Cathedral. Plaques around the inner courtyard garden record Clubland's famous associations. Today the clubs are gone but Clubland is put to good use, meeting the new needs of people from various cultural backgrounds.

Over the years Walworth has had many other churches. Two hundred years ago followers of the strange 'prophetess', Joanna Southcott, met at their 'House of God' at the Elephant and Castle. The old York Street Chapel has gone and the Beresford Street Chapel is no longer a place of worship. Behind the shops in Walworth Road may be seen the Sutherland Chapel, Liverpool Grove, erected in 1842 and closed in 1904. St Mark's, East Street, was destroyed in World War II. The 'Chapel Furniture' shop in Browning Street, which looks like a small church, was once its parish hall. Older people will remember the Baptist Church, on the site of the garage, 137 Walworth Road. For nearly 100 years Walworth also had a Jewish Synagogue.

When Walworth developed into a crowded inner-city area, with thousands of poor children needing education, the first free schools for them were started by the churches. The earliest of these, St Mary Newington, closed in 1965, but St Peter's, St Paul's and St John's, are still going strong. St Peter's had a school as early as 1839. It moved to its present buildings, in Liverpool Grove, in 1905. St Paul's School started in 1857. A school plaque, with the date, 1871, marks the site of its old building at 55 Sutherland Square. There was an extra infants' and junior school in St Albans Hall. The school bell, used there to call children to the start of morning and afternoon lessons, is in the Livesey Museum. St Paul's moved to its modern buildings in Penrose Street in 1956. St John's Schools, built at the same time as the church, opened in 1863. The children were taught mainly 'the 3 Rs', reading, writing and arithmetic, and the Christian religion, but it was not all work and no play. As early as 1869, there was a school outing. The children went by horse-drawn vans for a day at Chislehurst.

The very poorest of all children in Victorian Walworth, if they had any teaching at all, might have gone to a Ragged School, for example, the Richmond Street Ragged Schools, started by John Dunn in 1859. The teachers must have been especially dedicated, coping not only with ragged urchins but also with unhealthy smells. The school started in a loft over a disused cow-shed in East Street, then moved to Richmond Street, in an area where people went in for fish curing in their backyards, giving off what was known as 'otto (or odour) of haddocks'. Things were not much better when the school moved to rooms over a rag and bone shop! By 1875 it had a proper building, now the rear of East Street Baptist Church, though fortunately, soon after this, there was no longer a need for Ragged Schools.

In 1870 the government decided to make education available and compulsory for all children. The Education Act set up School Boards to provide sufficient schools. Many older schools in Walworth began as 'Board Schools'. These huge, solid, buildings often have, high up on the outside, an ornamental panel with the letters LSB, London School Board, the date the school was built, and its original name. Flint Street, erected in 1875, is now the English Martyrs Roman Catholic Primary School. It is built to the usual pattern for these schools, three storeys, originally for infants at the bottom, girls in the middle and boys on the top floor, with three separate entrances. Walworth School opened in 1946 as one of the London County

Council's first 'comprehensive schools', then a new idea in education. The upper school in Mina Road was built in 1965. The lower school's old board school plaque,reads 'Sandford Row School, 1891'. In 1990 when I.L.E.A., the Inner London Education Authority, was abolished, Walworth schools came under the Southwark Council Education Department.

In the past, those who had left school, but wanted to continue their studies, had no local colleges or even public libraries. In Walworth, however, from 1845 to 1881 ladies and gentlemen who could afford the subscription, could join the Walworth Literary and Scientific Institution, which had a library and reading room in Manor Place and a lecture hall in Carter Street. The Newington Working Men's Association, founded in 1854, also had a library and classes in such subjects as English grammar, arithmetic and French for men who probably had not had much chance of early schooling. The Robert Browning Settlement (see chap.10) was especially concerned with education. *The book of Walworth*, produced by their Adult Education Class, in 1925, is a valuable social survey of the Walworth of that period.

References and further reading

1. H.J.Bennett - *I was a Walworth boy*, pp 9-10, 32-42.
   Surrey Square and Mina Road Schools
2. L.J.Carter - *Walworth 1929-1939*, pp 54-59, 97-117.
   Flint Street and Paragon schools.
3. *The buildings of England, London 2. South*, pp 574-8.
4. *Survey* pp 95-104.
Books on individual churches include-
5. Douglas Bartles-Smith and David Gerrard - *Urban ghetto*, Lutterworth Press, 1976.
   The authors were clergy at St Paul's Lorrimore Square.
6. John D.Beasley - *The bitter cry heard and heeded; the story of the South London Mission*, 1889-1989, S.L.Mission, 1989. pp 147-151, 181-4.
   Former Methodist churches in Walworth.
7. M.Clifton - *The Southwark Martyrs*, Catholic Truth Society, 1980.
8. Mark Donovan - *A history of St Paul's, Lorrimore Square and St Agnes, Kennington Park*, privately publ. 1930.

9. Eric W.Hayden - *A centennial history of Spurgeon's Tabernacle*, Frost, 1962. Also many other books on Spurgeon.
10. Reginald Walter - *East Street Baptist Mission Walworth*, Invil 1959.
11. Rex Batten - *The Leysdown tragedy; an account of the deaths and funeral of eight Walworth Scouts in 1912*, Friends of Nunhead Cemetery, 1992.

10. SOCIAL PIONEERS

1908-88
80th Anniversary of Britain's first Old Age Pensions Act
Browning Hall (now Herbert Morrison House) was the headquarters of the National Committee of Organised Labour, which from 1898 until 1908 fought unceasingly until Britain's first Old Age Pension was won. Its principal leaders were the Rev.F Herbert Stead, Warden of the Browning Settlement and Honorary Secretary of the National Committee, and Frederick Rogers, Organising Secretary of the National Committee. Southwark Borough Council and the Pensioners' Forum today salute all who made this breakthrough possible and pledge to uphold the pensions' cause in our time.
Plaque on the outside of 195 Walworth Road.

Old people throughout Britain have reason to be grateful for a movement that began in Walworth, at the Robert Browning Settlement. The aims of the Settlement were set out as 'The furtherance of the Kingdom of God as it is declared in the Gospel of Jesus Christ, the amelioration of the life and lot of people dwelling in the Borough of Southwark and in other poor parts of London or elsewhere'. It provided free medical treatment and legal advice. It was a centre for social and educational activities involving thousands of local people. It had the largest 'Goose Club' in the country. Subscribers of a few pence a week could collect a goose or turkey and other goodies on Christmas Eve. Every year the Settlement sent 300 poor children for a fortnight by the sea. It still runs the Bethany Homes at Clacton for old people. The building which is now Herbert Morrison House was built in 1902 as the Browning Club and Tavern, an alternative to the local pubs, as the drink served was coffee!

But the first Warden of the Robert Browning Settlement, the Rev. Herbert Stead, saw there was one section of society who were treated especially unfairly, the old people who could no longer work. As he wrote, 'Many old people come to me begging for work, 'anything to keep me from the workhouse'. What kind of people are these? Not thriftless, but respectable, sober, honest, hard-working men and women who have brought up families, but in old age find themselves destitute. The moment someone ceases to be of value as an economic tool, they are flung aside as worthless'. Stead called a meeting at Browning Hall and four hundred people crowded in to hear a speaker from New Zealand talk about a government pension scheme already started in that country. Stead realised that only an Act of Parliament could bring about real improvement in Britain. So he began a nationwide campaign that was to go on for the next ten years. In 1899, a National Committee was formed with its headquarters at Browning Hall. Social reformer, Charles Booth, famous author of the 17 volume, *Life and labour of the people in London*, was one of the main supporters of the movement. He believed in tackling poverty by first collecting facts and figures, like a scientist. A plaque on the outside of the former Browning Tavern reads, 'Opened June 14, 1902, by Charles Booth, founder of the Science of Cities and by the Bishop of Hereford'. In 1908 victory was won. The government, under Prime Minister Asquith, with Lloyd George as Chancellor of the Exchequer, passed the first Old Age Pensions Act, allowing all people over 70 a state pension of five shillings a week; not much, but the principle had been established. From now on old people could proudly call themselves, 'not paupers but pensioners'.

The full title of Stead's committee was the National Committee of Organised Labour on Old Age Pensions. It consisted of representatives of Trades Unions, Trades Councils, etc. The Robert Browning Settlement became a centre of activity for the newly formed Labour Party. When Stead was Warden, Labour Weeks were held there annually. Speakers in 1913, included founders of the Party, Keir Hardie, and Ramsey Macdonald, later Britain's first Labour Prime Minister. In 1958 the Settlement building on

Walworth Road became the headquarters of the London Labour Party. It was renamed Herbert Morrison House after the statesman, Lord Morrison of Lambeth, one time President of the Robert Browning Settlement.

> English Heritage plaque
> Dr Charles Vickery Drysdale, 1874-1961,
> a founder of the Family Planning Association,
> opened his first birth control clinic here in 1921

Plaque on 153a East Street.

This plaque marks the site of another 'first' for Walworth, the first clinic in the country to offer medical family planning advice, a particular boon in its early years to Walworth women struggling to bring up over large families on low incomes. The clinic is now a Brook Advisory Centre.

Octavia Hill, a remarkable woman, founder of the National Trust, famous especially as a pioneer in providing better housing for working people, did some of her best work in Walworth. To see what she did, turn aside from the noise of Walworth Road into the comparative quiet of Merrow Street. In 1904, the Church Commissioners asked Octavia to help them redevelop their large estate of 22 acres east of Walworth Road. The land been let out on long leases, when it was just fields, and the leaseholders had allowed it to become an over-crowded slum. Fortunately, in 1904 the leases had run out. Under Octavia Hill's direction all the slums were demolished and replaced, not by great tenement blocks, but by the 2 storey cottages and 3 storey blocks of flats, which still make pleasant homes today. The cottages each have small back gardens and the flats look out on to garden courtyards, so the residents get as much fresh air and sunlight as possible.

Octavia Hill believed strongly that good housing should not only be provided but that it should be managed and cared for properly. This is obvious if you walk round the estate today, and see no vandalism or litter. The Estate Manager from his office in Merrow Street, uses the moderate rents, for repairs and internal modernisation, while keeping the buildings' distinctive outward appearance. Students of housing management and visitors from far afield come to learn from this estate in Walworth. It is the largest Church Commissioners' estate still managed by them in London and covers over 600 dwellings in Merrow Street, Burton Grove, Saltwood Grove, Worth Grove, Portland Street, and those added in the 1930's in Liverpool Grove. Date Street was purchased by Southwark Council some years ago. Octavia Hill also saw that the children had nowhere to play except the streets, and thanks to her the Church Commissioners gave Walworth the beginning of its first park, Faraday Gardens, east of St Peter's churchyard. The whole estate has been designated as the Octavia Hill Conservation Area.

References and further reading

1. *Eighteen years in the central city swarm*, W.A. Hammond, 1913. The Robert Browning Settlement, 1895-1913.
2. Robert Browning Settlement - Annual reports, etc.
3. Frances Stroud - *Recollections of the Robert Browning Hall and Settlement*, tape-recording, 1981.
4. *Municipal Journal*, 11th March 1904.
5. Gillian Darley - *Octavia Hill*, Constable, 1990, pp294-6.
6. Wendy Hill - *Walworth, seventy years on*, unpublished thesis, 1981.
7. Octavia Hill - *Extracts from Octavia Hill's letters to fellow workers*, 1864 to 1911, Adelphi Book Shop, 1933.

11. IMPORTANT BUILDINGS

One group of buildings in Walworth Road, between Larcom Street and Wansey street must be visited by practically all Walworth people at some time, as they house local government offices, library, and museum. They are worth looking at individually. The oldest, at the corner of Wansey Street, is the red brick and Portland stone, former Vestry Hall, of the local government parish of St Mary Newington. Its architect was Henry Jarvis. Notice its ornate Victorian decoration, the strange heads above the windows, and the columns of polished red granite. It must have looked even more impressive when it was first built, and stood alone. No doubt the Vestry

46

men felt proud when they marched from their old meeting place, St Mary Newington School, for the official opening on 8th August 1865.

It remained the Council Chamber and offices for Vestry staff for the next 35 years, during which there was certainly much work to be done by local government. In the 1860's Walworth could be a very unhealthy place to live in. Always damp and low-lying, it was being built up very rapidly without, at first, proper drainage or sanitation. In 1849, there had been a terrible outbreak of cholera. 'The land of death in which we dwelt was Newington', wrote Thomas Miller, a local poet. In 1857, the Medical Officer of Health for Newington reported on the 'large number of streets without main sewers where overflowing cesspools and choked drains have been emptied only to fill again'. Thanks to the efforts of the Vestry, conditions improved and R.W.Bowers could say in his book, *Sketches of Southwark old and new*, perhaps with some exaggeration, 'by 1900 Newington was one of the healthiest parishes in London'.

In 1900 the Metropolitan Borough of Southwark was formed by the amalgamation of four old parishes, Newington, St Saviour's (Southwark Cathedral), St George the Martyr, and Christchurch, Blackfriars Road. Newington Vestry Hall became the Southwark Town Hall, a meeting place for the Mayor and Council of the new Borough. The first Mayor, Arthur Dawes, Chairman of Newington Vestry since 1897, and later M.P. for Southwark has a street is named after him. The new Council included many who were already working for the good of Walworth, for example, five members of the Browning Settlement, Canon Jephson of St John's and Canon Horsley of St Peter's. Frances Stroud, who lived all her life in Larcom Street, and became Mayor in 1952 was one of a Walworth family devoted to public service. Her mother, father, and uncle were all members of Southwark Council. In 1965, the Metropolitan Borough of Southwark joined with Bermondsey and Camberwell to form the London Borough of Southwark. Camberwell Town Hall, Peckham Road, became the Town Hall for the large new Borough.

In 1993, Newington Library, next door to the old Vestry Hall, will be celebrating its centenary. It is so much part of the Walworth scene that those who use it probably just take it for granted. A hundred years ago, however it was only after a public campaign, with speakers using a wagon in Rodney Road as an open air platform, that local ratepayers were convinced of Newington's need for a library. Names of the Commissioners for Public Libraries, who were responsible for the building, are inscribed on the front. The official opening by the Princess Christian took place on November 30th 1893, a great occasion, with a guard of honour provided by the Queen's Royal West Surrey Regiment. When the library first opened there were books in the Lending Department but funds did not stretch to stocking the Reference shelves. Under the Metropolitan Borough of Southwark, Newington built up a fine Reference Department and in 1965, it became the Principal Reference Library for the London Borough of Southwark. Incidentally, the far-sighted first librarian, Richard Mould, was already, in 1893, appealing for any material on local history. It is thanks to him and later librarians that books such as the *Story of Walworth* can be compiled.

The third and latest of the group of buildings in Walworth Road is at the corner of Larcom Street. It was opened in 1937 by the Metropolitan Borough of Southwark as a Health Services Department. Above it are statues of a mother and children, showing it was particularly concerned with family health. The motto, 'The health of the people is the highest law', expressed the aim of the Borough Council, many years before there was a National Health Service. By 1918 Southwark had a Maternity and Child Welfare Committee which set up clinics for mothers and babies. The new building had a 'Solarium' which provided 'artificial sunlight', the best treatment known at that time for tuberculosis, the scourge of many poor families. Another service housed here was the Public Analyst's Department, set up to ensure the safety of food and drugs, which was only disbanded in 1991.

The very name, Manor Place, brings back memories to older Walworth people. Here were the famous Manor Place Baths, opened by Newington Vestry in 1898, as some of the finest in London. And what a boon they were to local people! As H.J. Bennett writes, 'Manor Place Baths for me meant having a decent bath in privacy. Friday night was bath night at home. The copper fire would have been lit in the afternoon and one by one we would be bathed in the oval washing-day bath in front of the kitchen fire with the water being topped up for the later ones. When I was about ten I was introduced to Manor Place Baths, and what luxury for a few pence. A long bath in which you could almost float and an unlimited supply of water. There were no taps inside. The attendant filled the bath sufficiently and tested it with his hand, shut the door and if you wanted more hot (or cold) you called out 'More hot (or cold) No.7', just like a lord addressing his valet.' But Manor Place was not just the place for a good wash. It had large swimming baths much used for swimming contests and water polo. In winter these were covered over for the famous Manor Place Boxing Tournaments where star boxers appeared in aid of charity. The baths finally closed in 1978 and only the facade and clock tower serve as a reminder of them. They were replaced by the Elephant and Castle Leisure Centre.

Behind the baths is the Manor Place Depot. The Refuse Department here was an early pioneer in recycling. In 1906 it installed machines to crush organic refuse into dust which was then sold to farmers in Kent to fertilise the soil! The great annual event at the Depot until 1936 was the Cart–Horse Parade. Seventy five of the Council's horses, all well groomed and harness shining, turned out for the Parade in 1905.

> Parish of St Mary Newington
> Electric Lighting Station

This stone was laid on 23rd September 1898 by Mr William Edwards, Chairman of the Electric Lighting Committee.
Plaque on 30 Penrose Street

Only seven years after the first public supply of electricity was switched on for the City of London, long before there was any National Grid or London Electricity, Newington Vestry set up its own Electricity Generating Station in Penrose Street. It was the first parish in South London so to do. Another stone reads,

The Cart–Horse Parade of 1905

Metropolitan Borough of Southwark
This stone was laid 6th October 1945 by Councillor Mrs Catherine Gates, Chairman of the Electricity Committee, to commemorate the rebuilding of these works after almost total destruction by a German flying bomb, 30th June 1944.

References and further reading

1. H.J.Bennett - *I was a Walworth boy.* p 23.
2. R.W.Bowers - *Sketches of Southwark old and new*, pp 39 and 493-5.
3. L.J.Carter - *Walworth 1929-1939*, pp 53-4.
4. Many press-cuttings, programmes of opening ceremonies etc.
5. *Horse brass*; the journal of the National Horse Brass Society, Dec. 1984.

For more advanced study-
6. *Minutes and Annual Reports of Newington Vestry, Metropolitan Borough of Southwark* and *London Borough of Southwark*.

12. 'EAST LANE' AND WALWORTH SHOPS

'East Lane', East Street Market, is famous throughout South London. Every day, except Mondays and Wednesdays, the narrow street is crowded with shoppers and, on Sunday mornings especially, bargain hunters come from far and wide.   There have long been stall-holders or 'costermongers' in Walworth. At first the barrows were not confined to the side streets but spread all along the main roads, Walworth Road, Old Kent Road, London Road and Newington Butts.   Probably they originally sold fruit and vegetables from the market gardens around Walworth. In fact costermongers meant 'mongers', or traders, who sold a variety of large cooking apples known as 'costard apples'. Later, of course, costers came to sell all kinds of goods, though East Street is still noted for its fresh fruit and vegetables. Before modern traffic, with the stalls lit by naptha flares, the costers crying their wares, and the crowds on a Saturday night out, the scene must have been even more lively than East Street is today.

Popular songs were written about the costers. The best known tells of a couple who were left a little donkey and cart by the wife's 'rich uncle Tom of Camberwell'. So they set off down Old Kent Road 'Like carriage folk' or 'the toffs as rides in Rotten Row' to the envy of their neighbours–
> 'Wot cher! all the neighbours cried,
> Who're yer goin to meet Bill?
> Have yer bought the street Bill?
> Laugh, I thought I should have died,
> Knocked 'em in the Old Kent Road!
Another song tells what you could buy in Walworth Road, for example,
> 'They've got cottons, they've got silks,
> They got winkles, they got whelks
> Orn the barrers in the Walworth Road!

According to the song-writer, there were even
>   '– canaries there all posh
>   What is sparrers when they're washed
>   Orn the barrers in the Walworth Road!'

From 1871, when tramlines were laid, the authorities tried to keep the barrows off the main roads as they caused too much congestion. There were many protests, but when electric trams replaced horse-drawn, the traders were finally forced to keep to East Street and Westmoreland Road. Even then, according to an article in the *Daily News* of 2nd November 1903, 'Southwark costers – are in revolt against the tyrants who have decreed their removal. As one of these 'martyrs' remarked, 'We were in London Road years afore electric trams was ever heard of and are we to get the push because there aint room for a police inspector to walk along flinging his arms abaht? Since some of us 'ave been in the side-streets we 'aven't sold more than six-pen'orth of carrots and a few bob's worth of taters a day'.

At first stall-holders in East Street and Westmoreland Road had no regular pitches. As Len Carter recalls, 'The market opened at 8.30am. No stalls or barrows emerged, even though waiting in the side streets, until a policeman gave them the 'tip', (by blowing his whistle). Then there was a grand rush for position'. Since 1927, market stall-holders have had regular pitches with licences from the Borough Council, for which they pay a weekly charge. Market Inspectors ensure there are no 'fly-pitchers', and rules say there must be at least four stalls between similar trades. Over the years, there have been some changes. There are no longer stalls selling day-old chicks and laying hens as when Walworth people lived in small houses, instead of flats, and kept chickens in their own backyards. At one time East Lane echoed to the cries of 'quacks' selling bottles of liquid guaranteed to cure all ills. The N.H.S. put them out of business. A traditional type of barrow from which thousands of children bought 'Genuine Ices Guaranteed' is now in the Livesey Museum. It belonged to Mrs Jones who traded in East Street for 65 years, taking over from her father before her. But traders still have the right to hand on their stalls to their next-of-kin, and some East Street families have been in business for a very long time. There has been a

Hugman's fish stall for over a hundred years and Rollo's ice-cream shop for nearly sixty. In changing times traders keep up the East Street traditions and are proud of them. No wonder many people prefer this real old London street market to any modern shopping centre.

Apart from the market, Walworth Road itself is one long shopping street, of mainly small shops, some with a long history. Baldwin's, founded by George Baldwin in 1844, was into natural remedies long before modern health movements. The window proclaims that it sells, 'Herbs, roots, barks, essential oils, gums, waxes, incense, flower remedies'. Inside you find shelves stocked, not with packaged medicines, but with old-fashioned glass jars and trays of herbs giving off an exotic scent. Baldwin's sarsaparilla drink, has long been famous as 'good for your blood'. The name-plate above Schwar & Co., Jewellers, is in old style gold lettering under glass. The

East Street Market 1992

business was established in 1838. The shops between Merrow Street and Liverpool Grove are part of quite a grand development, 'Erected AD 1908'. The pawnbrokers' sign of the three brass balls hangs above Harvey and

Thompson in Merrow Street and F.T.Gentleman in Walworth Road. As Len Carter recalls, 'Before the war Walworth had a good stock of pawnbrokers. Most frequented was Harvey and Thompson – Pawnbroking charges were reasonable, usually three farthings in the shilling per month. – Apart from when a housewife had to pawn her wedding ring, visiting 'Uncle' was quite respectable. Pawning suits, bed-linen, household goods, rings and watches was done frequently. Regular customers could be seen on Monday mornings on their way to deposit their bundles'.

Off the main roads, most back streets still have their corner shops. They were especially useful when no one had a fridge. Len Carter observes, 'All food was bought daily, – Everyone popped out for everything morning, noon and night'. If Davies' Dairy in Darwin Street, happened to be shut, you could still pop round for a 'pinta'. The door had a brass plate with a coin slot. A penny worked a 'brass cow' and released milk from a tap into the customer's jug. The shop and indeed much of the street has been demolished but the door, with its brass plate, is now in the Cuming Museum.

In the past, there were also many street traders who came round with such 'instant food' as hot potatoes. Len Carter recalls the muffin men. 'One could watch men making muffins at a tiny bakery in Elsted Street. When ready, three men, each with a tray of muffins, covered by a cloth, and balanced on a round pad on his head, and ringing a bell, set out to tour the streets. Their gait was rather stiff to avoid upsetting the balancing act.' In the Cuming Museum there are two old milk carts of local dairymen. Before there was bottled milk, Mr Rowling of Kennington brought his milk round in a big churn and delivered it to customers in small metal cans. A little later came milk in tall bottles with cardboard tops, as delivered by Martin Bros of Walcot Square. At one time there was even a pony and cart which went round the back streets with a small roundabout. Children could have a ride for the price of one penny or two jam-jars.

Shops in Newington Causeway, c. 1860

Then there were the 'Pearlies'. Costermongers had always believed in helping each other in times of trouble. From about 1880 a 'Pearly King' was chosen by the costers from each neighbourhood to dress up and go round regularly with his donkey and cart collecting for hospitals and other good causes. The mural on the outside of the North Peckham Civic Centre shows the Pearly King in his magnificent suit covered with pearl buttons, his wife, the Pearly Queen, her big hat decorated with brightly coloured ostrich feathers, and their children, the Pearly Prince and Princess. St Mary Magdalene Church, Massinger Street, now demolished, used to be the scene of the Pearlies' annual Harvest Festival.

Walworth once had some grand department stores to rival those of the West End. At the Elephant and Castle, there was no purpose-built Shopping Centre, but shop-window displays lining the streets to attract customers from far beyond Walworth. Isaac Walton & Co., 97-101 Newington

Causeway, a firm of men's and boys' outfitters advertised, in 1884, 'All our good quality garments cut and made up on the premises '. William Hurlock's, mainly for ladies fashions and also furniture, had premises on both sides of Walworth Road, north of the railway bridge. Burton's, the men's tailors, had a commanding site at the corner of St George's Road. War-time bombing and redevelopment have wiped out all trace of these buildings.

Old Kent Road once had at least two famous shopfronts. One was Edgington's, the tent, rope, sail and flagmakers, a firm founded in 1805, which had made flags for Nelson's flagship. When it closed in 1967, to make way for the Flyover, the shopfront was removed from 108 Old Kent Road to Woburn Abbey, where it is part of the Antiques Centre. There is a model at the Livesey Museum. Carter's, the other eye-catching shop, was at 211-217 Old Kent Road. Above the long shop-front was a clock and over it a Victorian gentleman wearing a bowler hat, which he raised on the stroke of every hour. The business, founded in 1851 by George Carter, sold clothes for men and boys and did so well that it soon had 30 shops across London. H.J.Bennett recalled some of the attractions of the Old Kent Road shop. 'To advertise their men's straw hats they had a moving line of horse-drawn carts with sheaves of corn going into a windmill with the sails turning'. Long before television, 'On Boat Race Day, scores of children would sit on the pavement outside Farmers, opposite Carter's, which displayed the light and dark blue flags, and cheer when the flag of the losing side was hauled down at the end of the race.' Carter's, finally closed in 1978. Farmers the drapers is now South London Pistons Ltd.

References and further reading
1. H.J.Bennett - *I was a Walworth boy*, chap. 3.
2. *Book of Walworth* , p56-60.
3. Len Carter - *Walworth 1929-39*, chaps. 7,8,13.
4. Alec Forshaw and Theo Bergstrom - *Markets of London*, Penguin, 1983.
5. Steven Harris - *Old surviving firms of South London*, Steven Harris, 1987.
6. *Tradesmen's bills*, 19th and early 20th century.
7. *Old Kent Road*, BBC2 Arena Programme, 1985.

13. NIGHTS OUT

No TV, no videos, not even radio, but Walworth people in the past had plenty of entertainment within walking distance of their own homes. For about fifty years, from about 1880 to 1930, many also came by train, tram or bus for a good night out at the music halls and theatres, for which the area was famous.

The first music halls were halls attached to pubs. By the 1890's, the Montpelier, earlier noted for its elegant tea-gardens, had a hall at the back seating 660 people, known as the Montpelier Music hall or the Walworth Empire. The South London Palace of Varieties, London Road, next to the site of the Bakerloo Underground Station, was one of the most famous of the great Victorian music halls. When first built in 1860, it was something new, a music hall not attached to a pub, but a purpose-built music-hall theatre. Rebuilt after a fire in 1869, it was a huge building seating 4,000 people. Most of the great 'old-timers' appeared at some time on stage here, for example Marie Lloyd, Dan Leno, George Leybourne. A play-bill for 7th September, 1885, lists a typical night's entertainment; performing dogs, champion skipping-rope dancers, Ali and Beni Arabian acrobats, Lollo, Lillo and Otto the 'bicycle wonders of the age', and 'the engagement regardless of expense of the greatest illusionist of the age Professor Carl Hermann' who produced' from nowhere in particular' two large live rabbits. At other times the 'South' put on ballets, or historic

South London Palace, playbill 1879

scenes, for example, Guy Fawkes and the Gunpowder Plot, or the Battle of Waterloo.

Not far from the South London there was the Elephant and Castle Theatre, New Kent Road, opened in 1872 on the present site of the Coronet Cinema. This was a real theatre for plays. Melodramas such as *Sweeney Todd the Demon Barber*, and *Maria Martin and the Red Barn* were very popular with its audiences. The Christmas pantomimes were great events,. At Christmas 1881, the pantomime was *Little Bo-Peep*, with a transformation scene, 'The Haunt of the Mermaid', a farmyard scene with real ducks, chickens, ponies and a donkey, and, as always in panto, a troupe of children. Long before the advent of television, the Elephant and Castle occasionally presented 'news pictures'. In July 1882, there was a *'Grand Panstereorama of Passing Events,* with fifty, colossal tableaux', illustrating the destruction of the Tay Bridge in Scotland and a battle in Zululand, South Africa. This was a theatre where ordinary people clearly felt at home. According to *Beneath the mask* by John East, the Elephant and Castle could be noisy and smelly with food and drink on sale in the bars and the audience constantly popping beer-bottle corks and eating fish and chips! Not to mention the 'prevailing odour of horses and leather' from the horse auction rooms nearly next door, (the famous London Horse Repository in New Kent Road).

The grandest of the local theatres was the Princess of Wales, later known as the Kennington Theatre, in Kennington Park Road, on the corner of Kennington Park Place. Built in 1892, it was described as 'the most beautiful theatre in London' with 'walls of Italian marble, paintings on the ceilings, and free use of gold leaf'. Plays presented here were top quality West End productions, for example, Ellen Terry in *Captain Brassbound's Conversion*, by Bernard Shaw, and Martin Harvey in *The only way*. At the opposite end of the scale were the 'penny gaffs', such as one in East Street, where the spectators, mainly youngsters, paid a penny each to sit on hard forms in front of a small makeshift stage, shouting their own comments on the action!

Walworth's rich theatre life was short-lived. The cinema arrived, and a night out for most people now meant the weekly, or twice weekly, visit to the 'pictures'. Many small cinemas sprang up along Walworth Road and Old Kent Road, often using older buildings. The former Sutherland Chapel, Liverpool Grove, became the Electric Theatre. Just south of it, in Walworth Road, was 'Jenkin's, and then, the Purple Picture Palace in Arnside Street. Two cinemas almost faced each other across Walworth Road near the railway bridge. The Montpelier, in its later years, was a cinema and there was another called the Gem in Carter Street. In 1914 there were three in Old Kent Road between Townsend Street and Mina Road and another at the corner of Trafalgar Avenue. All these were for silent films, before 'talkies' were invented. According to A.S.Hall, whose favourite cinema was 'Jenkins', 'As the words appeared (on the screen) the readers would read out loud each word, all at different speeds, which resulted in a mixed din'.

Soon picture-going became such a craze that big cinemas conforming to new safety standards, were built especially for that purpose. In Old Kent Road, just north of Leroy Street, there was the Globe, seating 1,200, and across the road, the Old Kent Picture House, seating 1,993, both erected in 1910. The big theatres, Kennington and the Elephant and Castle went over to films instead of, or as well as, live entertainment. Christmas, 1930 saw the opening of the grandest of Walworth's 'picture palaces', one of the largest cinemas in Europe, the famous Trocadero, New Kent Road, opposite the Elephant and Castle Theatre. It had seating for 3,394. The interior, was the height of luxury with 'softly shaded lights, rich carpets, soft beautiful upholstered chairs, gentle warmth and freshly washed air – and an impression of almost cathedral-like grandeur'. The programme 'three hours a week of forgetfulness', was continuous from noon to midnight, Mondays to Saturdays, with two feature films, cartoons, news, and sometimes live acts as well. One special feature of the 'Troc' was the magnificent Wurlitzer organ, shipped from America in 1930. Hidden below floor level when accompanying films, like all cinema organs, it was raised during the interval so that the audience could see and applaud the organist.

Trocadero, New Kent Road,1935

All Walworth's music halls, theatres and cinemas, except for the Coronet, are now a thing of the past. The South London Palace and the Kennington Theatre were both bomb-damaged in World War II and demolished soon after. The Globe and the Old Kent Picture House were demolished to build the Flyover. But already the days of the cinemas were numbered. There was television at home. The 'Troc' was bravely rebuilt in 1966 as the Odeon, but even this was demolished in 1988. Happily the wonderful organ was rescued by the Cinema Organ Society, and is now in the South Bank University, Borough Road.

Today there seems to be just one place left in Walworth for a 'night out'; the pub. In spite of changing scene, tastes and customers, many Walworth pubs, though rebuilt, have survived for well over two hundred years. In 1800 horse-drawn coaches were setting off almost hourly on weekdays, and also on Sunday afternoons, from the Red Lion, near Camberwell Gate, to take passengers to the City. At the same inn it was also possible to hire a post-chaise or even a 'glass coach' (for Cinderella?). The Horse and Groom, Walworth Road, goes back to the same period and originally had stables at the rear. Both inns are mentioned in *A companion from London to Brighthelmstone*. The Horse and Groom was last rebuilt in 1960.

There was a King's Head in Walworth Road when George III was king. The inn had a sign with his portrait over the entrance. In those days, the inn had a courtyard in front where customers could sit out on a summer evening, and there was a pump and a horse-trough round the corner in Manor Place. Visitors to the Surrey Zoological Gardens often called in for a drink. Lectures and concerts were held in the first floor Assembly Hall. The King's Head was rebuilt in the 1880's, and the Victorian pub extends over the former courtyard. The coloured tile picture to the side of the entrance, put in at this time, shows a scene from Shakespeare's play, *Henry VIII*; the King with Anne Boleyn. The Queen's Head, nearby in Amelia Street, was named in honour of George III's wife, Queen Charlotte. The Duke of Clarence, Manor Place, is another pub with a royal name. In 1830, the duke became King William IV. The fashion for royalty continued. Prince Alfred, second son of Queen Victoria, who became Duke of Edinburgh in 1866, that year had a pub named after him in Walworth Road. It still bears his portrait on its signboard.

A Crown and Anchor form part of the badge of the Royal Navy, a very appropriate sign for a pub at the corner of New Kent Road and Rodney Place, named after Admiral Rodney (1719-92). Names of both pub and street date from the days when his naval victories were in the news. The Lord Nelson pub, Trafalgar Street was named not long after Nelson's famous naval victory at Trafalgar in 1805. When the news of it arrived, there was already a pub called The Bell, in East Street. Old Kent Road has long been noted for its many pubs. Even now, counting both sides of the road, there are seven in the half mile between the Flyover and Albany Road. Some, however, have recently lost their historic names. Until a few years ago, The Gin Palace, on the east side of the road, was The Castle, the name by which an inn on this site had been known since at least 1745, when it was marked on Rocque's map. Another old map calls it Oliver Cromwell's Castle. It could have got its name from the fort erected near here in 1642 by the parliamentary side in the Civil War. The World Turned Upside Down nearby, has kept its 200 year old name.

Walworth's oldest pubs do not have buildings going back as far as their names, but some at least have grand Victorian buildings, for example, The Masons' Arms, which rises high above the small houses and shops of East Street. The date, 1898, is inscribed at first floor level, above the tools of the masons' trade, a pair of compasses and a mallet. An earlier Masons' Arms is listed in the London Post Office Directory of 1832. In the Old Kent Road, one of the most impressive buildings is the Thomas à Becket, rebuilt in 1898. A plaque on the outside recalls St Thomas à Watering, but regulars are probably not so much interested in the Canterbury pilgrims, or in the pub's Victorian architecture. For them it is the pub with the upstairs gym which has been the training ground of many famous fighters, names such as Henry Cooper, Mohammed Ali, Frank Bruno; the pub with the Boxing Museum.

And what happened to the most famous pub of them all, the Elephant and Castle? This was rebuilt at least twice, the last time in 1898. It was finally demolished in the redevelopment of the whole area after World War II. March 8th 1959, was the night for a last 'knees-up' before the last pint was pulled. A new Elephant and Castle, not far from the site, carries on the name.

References and further reading

1. L.J.Carter, *Walworth 1929-1939*, chap.17.
2. John East - *'Neath the mask*, Allen and Unwin, 1987. pp 113-226.
3. Diana Howard - *London theatres and music halls*, 1850-1950. Library Association 1970.
4. Peckham People's History - *The times of our lives*, Peckham Publishing Project, 1983.
5. Malcolm Webb - *The Amber Valley gazetteer of Greater London's suburban cinemas*, 1946-86.
6. The Local Studies Library has a large number of local play-bills.

Charlie Chaplin

A figure of Charlie Chaplin, the little man in the bowler hat and baggy trousers, is displayed on the pub of that name at the Elephant and Castle, as a constant reminder, is any were needed, of probably the best loved of all Walworth's notables. 'I was born on April 16th 1889 at 8 o'clock at night in East Lane Walworth', is how he begins his autobiography. His birth place was a room over the boot repairer's shop of his grandfather, Charles Hill. His parents had been married at St John's, Larcom Street. Both were in show-biz, appearing in the music-halls of South–wark and Lambeth,

CHARLIE CHAPLIN
(CHARLOT)   125

Charlie Chaplin, photograph courtesy of BFI

including the South London. They soon separated however, and Charlie's mother moved from one poor address to another. For a short time, when Charlie was four, he attended Victory Place School. His teacher remembered

his large eyes and dark curly hair. According to her, 'he copied his famou
walk from an old man who gave oatmeal and water to the horses with cab
and carts, outside the Elephant and Castle'. There is a blue plaque on 187
Kennington Road, where Charlie lived temporarily with his father. He wa
on stage from the age of seven. At seventeen he joined Fred Karno'
'Camberwell Fun Factory', a well-known group of entertainers, and with
them went to America to begin his career as a star of comic films.

Michael Caine
Michael Caine is the stage name of a present day film and TV star who was
brought up in Walworth. He and his parents, Ellen and Maurice Micklewhite
lived in Urlwin Street and later in Marshall Gardens, London Road, near the
Elephant and Castle. He went to John Ruskin School and then to Wilson's
Grammar School in Camberwell. His first taste of the cinema was at the
children's Saturday morning matinees at the Trocadero and his own first
attempts at acting and film–making were at Clubland.

Lloyd Honeyghan
Boxer Lloyd Honeyghan is from the Brandon Estate. Southwark gave him
a hero's welcome in 1986, when he returned from winning the World
Welterweight Championship in the U.S.A.

Harry Cole
For thirty years, 1952-82, Harry Cole was a popular and well-known officer
at Carter Street Police Station. His many books, which he is still producing,
give a humorous and vivid insider's picture of 'a policeman's lot'. He was
awarded the B.E.M. for his voluntary work. As a qualified F.A. coach he did
much to help local junior football teams.

Len Carter
Finally to Walworth's one real 'star'! In 1988 a minor planet, or asteroid,
between Mars and Jupiter, was named 'Len Carter', in honour of a true son
of Walworth, who became Executive Secretary of the British Interplanetary
Society, lecturer and writer of books on space travel, satellites, etc. Like
other Walworth notables, he came of a poor family. They lived in Barlow

Street and he went to Flint Street and later Paragon School, leaving at fourteen. Study, hard work, and a lifelong enthusiasm for astronomy, gained him his position, but he never forgot the Walworth of his youth of which he gives a detailed account in his book, *Walworth 1929-1939*.

References and further reading

1. Charles Chaplin - *My autobiography*, Bodley Head, 1964.
2. David Robinson - *Chaplin, his life and art*, Collins, 1985.
3. Harry Cole - *Policeman's progress*, 1980, *Policeman's lot*, 1981, and many similar titles. All publ. by Fontana.
4. James Dowsing - *Showbiz London*, Sunrise Press.
5. Michael Caine - *What's it all about?*, Century, 1992.

15. TWO WORLD WARS

Keyworth Street and Keyworth School are named after one of the heroes of the 'Great War', 1914-18, Lance-Corporal James Keyworth, of the 24th London, regarded by the old Metropolitan Borough as 'Southwark's Own Regiment'. In 1915, for great bravery in battle, he won the Victoria Cross, the highest military award. There was a procession in his honour from Braganza Street to Manor Place Baths. Sadly he died of wounds, in France, later the same year, aged only 22..

The unit he had joined had been formed originally in 1860 as a corps of the Surrey Rifle Volunteers. The Queen's, the regular regiment to which it was later attached, was much older, being named in 1661 in honour of Charles II's queen, Catherine of Braganza. The regimental badge of the Queen's, the Lamb and Flag, is still inscribed in stone over the unit's former headquarters in Braganza Street.

Keyworth came from Lincoln to join up. The names of Walworth's own native-born heroes may be less remembered, but the boys from the back streets signed on in their thousands at the Recruiting Office, set up at Walworth Road Town Hall, and went to fight for their country, many of them never to return. Their streets were proud of them. In September, 1915 the *South London Press* reported that Trafalgar Street, of only 120 houses 'holds the Empire record for recruits'. It eventually produced about 300 men for the armed services. By October 1916 there were 17 names on its Roll of Honour, displayed on the outside of one of the houses, surrounded by flowers in memory of those who had died. World War 1 was the first war in which those at home were in danger as well as those at 'the front'. In 1916 a Zeppelin dropped a bomb on Manor Place and in 1917 four people were killed by bombs in the Mina Road area.

In World War II, 1939-45, the whole of Walworth, on the route to central London, suffered enormously. The memorial on the outside of the Walworth Road Town Hall reads,

> 'In memory of 925 inhabitants of Southwark who lost their lives in the enemy attacks on London, 1939-1945'.

It also lists by name the members of the Civil Defence Services who 'gave their lives in the service of the community'.

Bombs which fell on Walworth were responsible for at least 445 of those killed. Many more suffered injuries. The Elephant and Castle subways were used as air raid shelters and others were constructed everywhere. One in Faraday Gardens could take 632 persons. Pullen's Estate shelter held 1,516. Sadly, the shelters were no defence against a direct hit and many were killed crowded together in them, for example, when the Flint Street shelter was hit on the night of 15th October, 1940. One of the worst disasters occurred on the 29th October, 1940 when St Peter's Church was hit. At least 64 of those sheltering in the crypt were killed. For those bombed out in air-raids, temporary Rest Centres were set up, for example, in Clubland, Surrey Square School, and Crossway Church.

Street patrols, rescue, and fire fighting, were organised from A.R.P. (Air-Raid Precautions) Posts, each covering a group of streets. Post 12, in Amelia Street, covered the streets between Walworth Road, Kennington Park Road, and Penrose Street. The Post Warden, J.H.Barham, was awarded the George Medal, for bravery in rescuing people from the First Aid Depot in

Bomb damage, Newington Causeway,1941

Crampton School when it had a direct hit. This is how his Deputy Warden, A.H.Pullin, described another night of the Blitz, 10th May, 1941. 'St Mary's Church had caught fire and burned like a torch, the rose window in the east wall filled as with glass of the brightest mediaeval orange. – At the Elephant and Castle a major conflagration was developing. In Walworth Road, Newington Butts, St George's Road, New Kent Road, Borough Road and London Road, shop after shop was consumed. Bands of fire spread from side to side of the roads and sweeping from end to end, destroyed all in their path. The A.F.S. (Auxiliary Fire Service) were unable to get water from their hydrants. Clouds of red-hot embers rained down and the roar of flames and crashing of falling walls was continuous. Dawn broke but still the H.E.s (High Explosives) fell. —At last at 05.54 the all-clear came.' In five months, January to May 1941, Post 12 dealt with 14 H.E.s, 3 U.E.B.s (Unexploded

Bombs) and 2,385 incendiaries.

Many school children were evacuated during the war. A teacher at the Southwark Central School, which was in West Square, kept a detailed photographic record of her school's evacuation to Newton Abbot, where inner city girls learnt of life on Devon farms.

Walworth men and women, meanwhile, were serving in all the main fields of the war. The 24th London Regiment of the Queen's was at Dunkirk, Alamein, Salerno, and the Normandy landings. Lt. Colonel Macwilliam, a Commanding Officer, serving with the 8th Army, was awarded three D.S.O. medals and a Military Cross. The Queen's War Memorial in Kennington Park, lists the unit's battle grounds in two World Wars.

References and further reading

1. John Hook - *The air raids on London during the 1914-18 war*, No.14, *The raids on Southwark*, privately publ., 2nd ed. 1989.
2. *Territorial battalions of the regiments of Surrey and their successors, the Queen's Regiment*, Queen's Regimental Museum, Clandon Park, 1988
3. *Civilian war dead 1939-45; Southwark*, Imperial War Graves Commission 1954.
4. A.H.Pullin - *The story of Reporting Post 12 1938-44*, Privately publ.,1944
5. Southwark Borough Engineer's Dept - *Shelter accommodation*, 1940.
6. Southwark Central School - *Material on evacuation, World War II*.
7. J. A. Pester - *Recollections*, tape 5, *the Blitz*. Tape-recording.
For further research
8. J. M. A. Tamplin - *The Lambeth and Southwark Volunteers,1860-1960*, Regimental History Fund, 1965.
9. *Southwark Incident Registers*, 1940-43, and other records, Southwark Archives 5914-6.

6. A NEW WALWORTH

If someone who left Walworth fifty years ago were to pay a return visit today, he or she would find much of it almost unrecognisable. On the ground, once familiar small streets have completely disappeared, while towering above, are buildings about four times the height of any seen before World War II. The area of greatest change is at the Elephant and Castle. The war had left it devastated. The London County Council completed the transformation by declaring a whole thirty acres around the Elephant a Comprehensive Development Area. The aim was, first, to get rid of traffic jams, long a problem here. As most of the area was already flattened, a drastic solution was possible. The street pattern itself was changed, and new subways were constructed for pedestrians. The long island between Newington Butts and Walworth Road, site for the past two centuries of the Elephant and Castle pub and the Drapers' Almshouses, disappeared for road widening. Two smaller, traffic islands were created. The aluminium 'silver box' on the north island is an electricity sub-station for the Underground. It was designed to look like a dynamo as a memorial to Michael Faraday, near where the electricity pioneer was born.

The Elephant and Castle Shopping Centre, the central feature of the Development Area, opened in 1965. It had been planned, on what was then the latest American model, to be one of the largest such centres in Europe. In its early years, it proved not so successful as its L.C.C. planners had hoped, but, recently, under the London Borough of Southwark, has had a 'facelift', and is now surrounded with lively market stalls. The subways leading to it have been improved with better lighting and colour murals. Some show characters from Southwark history and local events; others such far away places as tropical forests and coral seas.

All around the Elephant and Castle arose large buildings, constructed of concrete, in the style favoured by architects of the 1960's, totally unlike those destroyed by Hitler's bombers. Alexander Fleming House, Newington Causeway, is by the architect, Erno Goldfinger. The London College of Printing and Distributive Trades, which moved to its new headquarters at the Elephant in 1964, is now one of the largest colleges in Europe for the study of creative media and communications. The tower block of the Draper Estate on the west of the road junction was the tallest block of flats in London when completed in 1964. More recent buildings are in the style and materials of the 1980's and 1990's, for example, in Newington Causeway the British Technology Group headquarters, in brick and glass, and the office block in granite, glass and steel, by the Swedish developers Ak Larson, in partnership with Southwark Council, leased in 1992, by the Department of Health . There are only three survivals from the Elephant and Castle of pre-war days; the Metropolitan Tabernacle, a welcome landmark in a sea of modern buildings; the Bakerloo Underground Station with, above it, what were once the offices of the South London Press; and finally, of course, set up outside the Shopping Centre, the actual sign of the Elephant and Castle, which was removed from the roof of the old pub when it was finally demolished.

Like the Elephant and Castle, the road junction where Old Kent Road meets New Kent Road, Tower Bridge Road, Tabard Street and Great Dover Street had long been another scene of traffic chaos. In 1970, this large area was also cleared for road improvement, by the Greater London Council. The Bricklayers Arms Flyover, 1500 feet long and 25 feet wide was built to take southbound traffic. Here too attractive older buildings disappeared, notably the pub which gave the Flyover its name, and the Old Kent Road Library at the junction with New Kent Road, which was replaced by the 'shop library' at the corner of East Street.

South of the Elephant, huge housing estates, the homes of large numbers of Walworth people, are the most noticeable feature of the landscape today. They came about as a result of the massive redevelopment schemes of the 1950's, 60's and 70's. Much building was necessary to replace houses lost through wartime bombing, or by demolition in slum clearance schemes begun before, and continued after, the war. There were long waiting lists for housing. Planners at that time believed the way to meet housing needs was to build upwards. They went in for wholesale clearance of large areas, replacing little streets and small houses with sky-high buildings surrounded by public open space.

The London County Council's architects designed the white tower blocks of the Brandon Estate, six of 18 storeys and five of 25 storeys; though the estate also includes houses and maisonettes of more normal height, and its own Brandon Library and Community Hall. The estate even has its own important work of art, *Reclining Figure,* by the famous sculptor, Henry Moore. Seen against the background of Brandon's tall towers even this strange giant in stone seems cut down to size.

By the late 1960's a new material was available for high-speed, instant building, pre-cast concrete slabs, ready-made in a factory. The enormous Aylesbury Estate, designed by Southwark Council architects, has 2,434 dwellings and about 8,000 residents, as many as the whole population of a small town. With ever increasing traffic, planners of the Aylesbury built high walkways for pedestrians, separating them entirely from the motor car. Even the shops are above ground level. It was not realised, at first, that these walkways might also have their hidden dangers. The estate was planned to provide for most immediate needs of the residents, with day nursery, hall, day centre, health centre, and green open spaces sheltered by the high blocks from traffic noise. The Heygate Estate, stretching from Walworth Road across to New Kent Road is similar to the Aylesbury but about half as big, with 1,194 dwellings.

Walworth also has modern housing of a very different kind. After the Aylesbury and the Heygate, no more huge estates and tower blocks were planned. The Council, and also private developers, took note of the type of homes most families like to live in, and built low blocks and small houses with gardens. Once again bricks were used, as in years gone by. Often, however, the houses do not face on to the street but their front doors open on to footpaths and traffic-free courtyards. When exploring Walworth take a walk round some of these pleasant looking developments, such as Newington Estate off Newington Butts, Pasley Close off Penrose Street, Langdale Close off John Ruskin Street, Penton Place and the west end of Manor Place.

References and further reading

1. B.Cherry and N.Pevsner - *The buildings of England; London 2 South.*
2. *London Borough of Southwark permanent housing estates,* L.B.S. 197€ also brochures on individual estates and buildings.
3. Tony Parker - *The people of Providence; a housing estate and some of its inhabitants,* Hutchinson, 1983.
   Based on tape-recordings on the Brandon Estate.
4. Timothy Richardson - *The Elephant and Castle Comprehensive Development Area,* 1955-65, and *The Elephant and Castle and its Shopping Centre,* unpubl. theses, 1979.
5. *Walworth Walk,* L.B.S. Development Dept. 1980.

17. WALWORTH'S PEOPLES

The 1981 census recorded 31,464 people as then living in Walworth. Ir some ways the residents have much in common. Most are ordinary working people. Certainly few would describe themselves as very rich The sound of their voices suggests that many are from old South Londor families who have lived here for generations. Walking through East Stree or along the crowded pavements of Walworth Road, as shoppers look fo bargains or stop to chat with neighbours, even a stranger would feel they are a warm and friendly people. Perhaps this is why newcomers of so many races and countries have been accepted and seem able to make their homes peacefully in Walworth. For it must be one of the most cosmopolitan places in London. In Walworth road, the Continental Delicatessen, with a shop sign in Greek, is not far from the Turkish Market. Within easy walking distance, Italian, French, Indian, Indonesian, Malaysian and many Chinese restaurants, tempt the diner-out.

Walworth residents include a cross-section of people from all over the world. The most obvious evidence of this is, of course, in the colour of their skins, whether black, white, yellow, or shades of either; but much more interesting are their individual ethnic origins. Among the facts given by the 1981 Census is 'Birthplace of Head of Household'. In the three wards, Newington,

Browning and Faraday, 818 of every 1,000 were born in the United Kingdom, 63 in the Irish Republic, 90 in the New Commonwealth and Pakistan, 29 in the rest of the world. But people have been settling in Walworth for a very long time and many of those 'born in the UK' could have had parents or grandparents born overseas. A Roman Catholic Chapel where Irish people could worship was opened in London Road in 1790. (Later the site of the South London Palace). It was replaced in 1848 by St George's Roman Catholic Cathedral. An eminent doctor, Cecil Belfield Clarke, born in Barbados, had his surgery for 50 years in Newington Causeway, until he died in 1970. The large influx of West Indians began, however, in 1948 when the *Empire Windrush* docked at Tilbury, bringing 492 Jamaicans to work in this country. They were accommodated at first in the Clapham Common Deep Air Raid Shelters. Many have since then settled in the Southwark area.

Organisations based in or around the Walworth area give an indication of its mixed population. The Southwark African Organisation, the South Asian Women's Organisation, and the Afro-Asian Advisory Service are all based in Camberwell Road. The Pan-African Organisation and the Southwark Employment Development Division, (a business advisory service for ethnic minorities), are located on the Aylesbury Estate. Clubland has an Advice Centre for those from other countries wishing to apply for British nationality and houses a churches' unit concerned with racial justice. In Bethwin Road there is the Umoja Theatre which 'aims to educate the public of multi-racial Britain in the art of the theatre and other arts.'

It is the organisations catering for special smaller groups which really throw light on individual countries from which Walworth's people come. There is a Bengali Women's Group on the Rockingham Estate, just north of New Kent Road. Their homeland is Bangladesh. The Black Women's Action Group in Elsted Street sets aside a day a week for women from Somalia. There are enough Vietnamese, to have their own advice sessions at the Citizen's Advice Centre in Walworth Road. A Kurdish Women and Children's Association meets at Cambridge House, Camberwell Road. There is an association in East Street, for women from Mauritius, that small island in the Indian Ocean.

Religious congregations give another insight into Walworth's multi-cultura population, though they may have members from a wider area. Chines Christians hold services in Cantonese at Clubland Methodist Church. Th church's main services, in English, attract many Methodist Christians fror West Africa. The two Pentecostal churches, which also use this buildin , consist mainly of Afro-Caribbeans. The New Testament Assembly hold services at St Paul's, Lorrimore Square. The former All Saints Churcl Surrey Square, is now 'The Church of the Lord (Aladura)', founded in Nigeria. The former Lady Margaret Church, Chatham Street, is now 'Th Mount of Salvation of the London Branch of the Eternal Sacred Order o Cherubim and Seraphim', which also uses the former Methodist church in Oakley Place. St Mary's Greek Orthodox Cathedral is in Camberwell Nev Road. Muslims have an Islamic Mosque and Cultural Centre in Harpe Road, off Newington Causeway. Rastafarians meet in St Agnes Place Kennington Park Road.

Peoples with these richly diverse origins, cultures and faiths, may feel, a yet, that their roots are elsewhere, reminders of the long and proud historie of their ancestors are far away. But, as years go by, they too are making thei own special contribution to the history of Walworth.

References and further reading

1. *Southwark Local Organisations File*
   Available in Newington Reference Library, Walworth Road.
2. *Census 1981: Small area statistics*, OPCS 1983.
3. Alo-War, Black Women's Oral History Group - *Our story*, Willowbrook Urban Studies Centre, 1990.
4. *Forty winters on; memories of Britain's post-war Caribbean immigrants*, Lambeth Services, The Voice, South London Press, 1988.
5. *So this is England*, 1984, and other books by Peckham Publishing Project

8. A PALIMPSEST OF THE PAST

> Palimpsest - a manuscript on parchment from which the original writing has been erased, and another text written over it. However, the ink of the old writing penetrated so deeply that even severe scraping could not remove all traces of the first text.

Set between the lines of two Roman roads, recorded in documents for over a thousand years, Walworth today, unlike some country towns, or even some other London villages, shows few obvious signs of its long history. Partly this is because Walworth is a place for people, a place where life must go on. It has its listed buildings and conservation areas, and even its own museum, but is certainly not somewhere where time has stood still. In the 20th century it has also suffered hard knocks from war-time bombing and post-war redevelopment. And yet, if you look more closely, you can, in fact, find many reminders of Walworth's past. It is rather like a palimpsest, a document which, with the right treatment, reveals what was written there before.

Manor Place is a turning off Walworth Road which led, in the Middle Ages, to Walworth Manor House. St Mary Newington was last rebuilt after World War II, but is in direct line from a parish church going back nearly 800 years. The street pattern of Walworth Road and East Street dates from the time when they were the centre of a country village. The sign of the Elephant and Castle goes back well over 200 years and many other pub and street names recall the past. The barrows of 'East Lane' have attracted generations of shoppers.

The homes of present day Walworth people are another link with the past. It is true no Tudor cottages have survived, such as must once have been seen in 'Walworth Street', but there are houses in Surrey Square and Kennington Park Road where the first residents moved in over 200 years ago. Traffic was still horse-drawn and Queen Victoria was on the throne when many of Walworth's small streets were laid out. Other local residents view the whole of Walworth, and indeed London, from tower blocks in the revolutionary new style of building used to rehouse people after World War II. And some Walworth people are themselves the first residents of the small new houses of today.

More research could well be done on Walworth. It has not attracted as much attention from scholars and writers as some, perhaps, 'posher' places. But if you are one of those who live there, you can take pride in its rich and varied history, and in a place that is full of life today. The *Story of Walworth* does not end here. The next chapters are up to you.

This book was produced by the London Borough of Southwark Local Studies Library; Librarian, Nicola Smith, Archivist, Stephen Humphrey.

Text by Mary Boast.

Illustrations are from photographs and prints in the Local Studies Library.

Published by the Council of the London Borough of Southwark, 1993
First published in 1976. Enlarged and rewritten 1993
Printed by Southwark Print

London Borough of Southwark Neighbourhood Histories

1. The Story of Camberwell
2. "   "   " Dulwich
3. "   "   " Peckham
4. "   "   " Walworth
5. "   "   " Bermondsey
6. "   "   " Rotherhithe
7. "   "   " 'The Borough'
8. "   "   " Bankside.

Southwark
Council

Price £3.00